Practical Parenting for

Muslims

BY NORMA TARAZI
2020

First Edition

ISBN: 978-0-578-70154-7

Cover art by Falah Shwan

Table of Contents

Preface

This is the book I wanted when my first child was born in 1979. I've spent much of my life since slowly accumulating the information to write it.

My mother laid the groundwork for my study. My mother, and the women of my family, all college graduates, were among the generation of parents who read the latest in scientific studies on child development and psychology that emerged following World War II in the United States. In my family we don't blindly follow tradition. We raise our children following the latest theories in child development and education. My mother showered me with books on parenting and child development. But I converted to Islam and I needed a book on parenting that for Muslims, derived from Qur'an and Sunnah, and expressed in everyday language with examples.

In 1995 my first book, *The Child in Islam*, was published by American Trust Publications (ATP), a publishing branch of the Islamic Society of North America. It was the result of a general project I started with friends from an Islamic study group for converts that was held in Kuwait, where I lived before the Gulf War. Our goal at the time was to gather as many quotes from Qur'an and hadith as we could find that we felt were related to raising our children. We wanted to understand from them how to change our child-raising methods to follow Islam rather than the way we were raised. With the war we were all separated and I ended up home in the States with all the material the group had gathered. I continued the research and finally put together a book and had it published.

A lot happened after publication. I continued my studies in education and Islam. I spent several years teaching adults about Islam at my local mosque and then worked as a middle school math and science teacher. I also became a grandmother and spent several years working in daycare settings.

Seeing my grandchildren growing up and watching the changes in the Muslim community, I sensed that the information in my early book was still needed but not generally available. I also felt that it needed to be updated and revised to be more useful. To that end I asked some young mothers among my friends to read through it and give their advice and suggestions. Emily Secan, Hoda Yousef, Nadia Yousef, and Amina Musa, all mothers of young children, spent several months reading the book and suggesting many updates, along with my friend Freda Shamma. In the end, I simply started over and wrote this new book, containing much of the same material but including more topics with better organization and streamlining.

Dr. Asma Mobin-Uddin, pediatrician and author of several popular children's stories about Muslim children, read through the whole draft of the book and gave me many ideas for improvement. My husband, Dr. Mouhamed Nabih Tarazi, who has worked as an imam and community leader for years, read the new book for content and helped with questions of Arabic translation. Hiba Nasser did much of the editing. Falah Shwan did the wonderful picture for the cover. I'm very grateful for all their help.

Learning about parenting is not useful in and of itself. If I don't change how I deal with my family, the knowledge is useless. In implementing my learning to try to become a better mother, I personally have always found strength in remembering the hadith: *"Do good deeds properly, sincerely and moderately and know that your deeds will not make you enter Paradise, and that the most beloved deed to Allah is the most regular and constant even if it were little."* (Bukhari) So I tried to take on one issue at a time, the most important among the issues, and work on fixing that. Then I went on to other issues. I have not been perfect as a mother, but I've done my best and may Allah cover my errors and faults and magnify my small successes.

I pray to Allah that this book may bring only good to parents and their children, and that He protect them from any mistakes or misunderstandings.

A few notes on vocabulary:
Islam, like Christianity and other faiths, has some words that have specific meanings, like salah and du'a mean specific forms of prayer. I've used Islamic terms because they are much clearer than alternative terms. The word 'prayer', for example, can conjure up imagery that is different from

one person to another, depending on that person's background. I've generally put explanations for these terms in the text, close to where the word is first introduced, and sometimes if the word is used again much later, so a glossary is not needed.

For the book's non-Muslim readers: I have chosen to use the word "Allah" throughout the book instead of the word "God". All quotes of Qur'an are from *The Holy Qur'an in Today's English* by Yahiya Emerick, but with this word change. The words are interchangeable in English for Muslims, but I and all of the people who helped me in this project have the habit, indeed, we have the love of referring to Allah.

I have used the following abbreviations after the names of Allah, prophets, and companions of Prophet Muhammad (s), a tradition in Muslim writing:

(swt) - an abbreviation for an Arabic phrase which means approximately "may He be glorified and praised".
(s) - an abbreviation for an Arabic phrase that means "peace be upon him".
(r) - an abbreviation for an Arabic phrase that means "may Allah be merciful with him/her."

Hadith: records passed down by the companions of Prophet Muhammad. They consist of the Prophet's sayings and actions, often with bits of information about the circumstances, why these sayings or actions occured. There are 6 main collections of hadith in the Sunni tradition of Islam, Bukhari, Muslim, Tirmidhi, Abu Dawud, Ibn Majah, and An Nasa'i. The scholars who collected these sets had different criteria for each of their collections.

Sunni: following the Sunnah, or example of the Prophet, this term is used in opposite to the term Shii. The Muslim community is divided roughly into two groups though not of equal size. The main group, with about 80% of all Muslims, are the Sunni, and the second group, located primarily in Iran and parts of Iraq, follows a political succession of leadership of the Muslim community traced through the descendants of Ali, son-in-law of the Prophet and husband of the Prophet's daughter Fatima, rather than the leaders selected by the Muslim community.

INTRODUCTION

Each day, some people take *shahadah* and accept Islam as their new way of life. They place themselves and their families in the situation of adapting the various aspects of their lives to their new faith. All their inclinations as parents, passed down to them from their own parents and social groups, are called into question. What is Islamic and what isn't? How do we go about implementing new Islamic concepts and behaviors into our lives and getting rid of behavior that conflicts with Islam?

At the same time, the Muslim world is in a state of tremendous upheaval from wars and migration and dealing with how to respond to the challenge of secular culture. People born into Muslim families all over the world are asking similar questions, faced with raising their children in a modern world, where remaining Muslim and practicing Islam face new complications. Culture and Islam were traditionally merged in most Muslim countries. What is Islam and what is culture? What must be preserved and what can be altered or adapted?

The family taught how to celebrate Eid and how to pray as part of the family identity. The village or neighborhood reinforced these teachings. Then social upheaval tore down the old system and families have been working to adapt to new environments. What old cultural traditions will still be maintained in the new world the family is in now? Islamic education and faith practice need to be separated from the old culture and reimagined in the new. There is a great deal of sorting out to be done.

If our goal is to raise our children to grow into adults who have faith and practice Islam, there is a lot of advice floating around, but in bits and pieces. Grabbing a bit here and a piece there can create odd results, like the young man from a Muslim home who always insists that his meat be halal, but he moved into an apartment with his girlfriend and has no interest in marriage. Another example would be the girl who wears hijab and prays most of the five prayers, but she acts rudely to everyone, including her parents, and she lies so often, no one can trust her. How do all the bits and pieces of child-raising advice fit together to create a system that makes sense and actually produces well-rounded practicing Muslim adults? That is the challenge that is being addressed in this book.

We need both the overview of the forest and an understanding of the trees in that forest so we can attempt to put a coherent system of child-raising together in our own lives with our own families. We also need the ability to evaluate all the new modern advice on child-raising and see what compliments our world-view and what would be in conflict with it and should be ignored.

All families have some problems raising their children, even if both parents are in the home and they agree a lot with each other. Often today there are additional complications for a parent. There is divorce and children are with a single parent or the children pass back and forth between parents, who differ in their interest in Islamic education. Maybe one parent is Muslim and the other is of another faith. Parents may have been non-practicing Muslims for years but now decide to return to faith practice when their children are older, so there has been little to no Islam in the home. Maybe the parents are new converts with older children.

Allah (swt) knows our circumstances and each step we take toward Him will be rewarded. Do small things regularly and expand out from there when you can. Allah knows the magnitude of responsibility that falls on the single parent and the one with few relatives around to help. The reward for these parents is great. The Muslim community also has a responsibility to support parents in these situations. When we have an overview of our goals, we have targets to aim for. Small steps may seem insignificant and a goal unattainable, but even the best of situations will never be perfect. If we strive forward for Allah, He will assist us in unexpected ways. The grouchy rebellious teen we fear lost for good may grow into a responsible Muslim parent himself one day. It happens.

Older children and adults have a different growth process in Islam than a young child does, but it's an ongoing process for everyone. The details change for older youth, but the atmosphere of gentle learning should be the same for all. There is no compulsion in religion and people have varying priorities. We need to adjust our expectations to the specific situation of each person.

For example, one person with a calm and supportive family life can work on achieving greater closeness to Allah through spending part of Ramadan in i'tikaf, a kind of camp-in at the mosque for a few days of prayers and devotional activities, while another with a hectic life finds challenge in just trying to get through the minimum basic faith rituals and working to control their anger. Allah knows the circumstances of each and rewards each one based on the effort and the degree of difficulty faced. We shouldn't judge one superior to the other.

The first step toward learning Islamic parenting is to define what relationships the child has with Allah and with his or her parents. We look to the Qur'an and hadith for these definitions, which will be covered in Chapters 1 and 2. These definitions can be different in different faiths and cultures and many decisions about how to manage children grow out from these definitions.

Chapters 3 through 5 organize our parenting teaching methods into modeling, rewarding positive behavior, and direct instruction techniques. In Chapter 6, strategies for dealing with problems are covered in the order in which they should be considered, depending on the nature of the problem. All of these methods are drawn from the example of Prophet Muhammad (s) and how he taught. Chapters 7 and 8 progressively broaden out the child's world by adding extended family and community relationships. The child has relationships not just with parents and siblings but also with their extended family, grandparents, aunts and uncles, cousins, and with the larger community. These relationships may be defined differently from how they are defined by other societies. We need to appreciate these relationships and encourage them where we can. They are different in their importance from the relationships in secular and other lifestyles.

The only relationship which really changes for the child as he or she grows up is that of accountability to Allah. Children aren't held accountable for their actions before reaching the age of understanding. All other relationships may develop and deepen as the child grows. But no matter our age, we always need to honor our parents, show respect to our elders, be gentle with the younger ones, and honor family ties. These relationships continue for a Muslim throughout his or her life.

Chapter 9 at the end of this book presents the few traditional activities Muslims do in response to a birth, following the example of the Prophet. All of these fall into the category of Sunnah (following the Prophet's example in word or deed or what he approved of in others).

Aside from these few simple practices carried out when a baby comes into the world, Islam has no ceremonies devoted exclusively to children – no first communion, no coming-of-age celebrations. Children are not segregated into a special world separate from that of adults; rather they are members of extended families in the great, embracing cycle of human life.

The family supports them when they are young, they support the family in their productive years, and in old age they are again supported by the family. They should grow and develop gradually in a system that encourages growth and learning, but places little emphasis on milestones and anniversaries. People can mark milestones with little celebrations if they want, like when a child learns her first surah or grandma and grandpa return from Hajj, knowing that these are fun things to do but nothing is required so we have a lot of flexibility. A general rule is: if good things happen to you—a promotion at work, a school graduation, you recover from surgery—thank Allah and share with others from the wealth He has given you, and avoid excess.

1 - THE CHILD AND THE SPIRITUAL WORLD

How we define the child makes a difference in how we treat him or her. If we believe that the child was born sinful—and view our job as one of civilizing this child, (the European Christian view for many centuries), we may always be looking for the bad and punishing. But this is a false picture and it will lead us in the wrong direction in raising our children. Another image people may pick up in general society is that humans are made in the image of God. This is not an Islamic teaching either.

Say (to them): "Allah is the one and only, Allah, the only one to turn to for help. He has no child, nor was born from a parent, and He is not like anything else." (Qur'an, 112)

Allah created each child pure, free of sin, and gave the child a soul. From birth the child is in submission to Allah and follows His guidance, as do all other living things.

Our Lord is the One Who gave each thing its natural disposition, then gave (it) guidance. (Qur'an 20:50)

All who reside within the heavens and the earth bow down before Allah, either willingly or unwillingly, as do their shadows in the mornings and the evenings. (Qur'an 13:15, also 16:49-50)

Fitra

Every living creature is created with fitra. The fitra of a living creature is its inborn nature, disposition, and characteristics. It knows the way Allah intended it to live. It's more than instinct. It is the total make-up of the person or animal according to Allah's design and it is in total submission to Allah from the instant of creation. For a human, we are expected to know right from wrong and will be held accountable for our choices by Allah (SWT) only from the age of puberty, or the age of understanding.

12

We know babies reach out for their mothers first and bond with them. It is part of the natural makeup of the baby and mother to do this. A child has a natural program inside that makes her struggle over months to control her body and pull herself upright to walk. A baby starts with smiling at his parents. They respond. He starts making sounds and gradually learns to control the sounds that come out of his mouth. Soon he has mastered his parents' language. In the same way children are made ready to wonder about the world and learn about their Creator. The religion that best fits with the fitra of a child is Islam.

No baby is born but upon Fitra. It is his parents who make him a Jew or a Christian or a Polytheist. (Muslim)

It is through our fitra that we feel the presence of Allah, that we search for justice and truth in the world, and that we love and care for others and feel our unity with all creation.

Another part of fitra is the inclination of the child to look to his or her parents for guidance in the world. That doesn't mean the child accepts guidance passively. Children test the limits, question, and rebel often as they grow. But Allah has made them recognize and even idealize their parents as role models for them. This makes parents the ideal teachers to guide a child to Allah.

Allah (swt)

Learning about Allah is a natural desire in children. They want to know where He is, what He looks like, and compare Him to Superman and other beings they have heard of. We need to answer carefully so they get good, dependable information. It's not a traditional Islamic metaphor, but in talking to young children, some people compare Allah to the wind, which can be felt but not seen. It's everywhere and it can be strongly felt when it is blowing the trees and other things around, or it can be quietly in the background, just taking care of our need to breath without us noticing. The Qur'an gives us many examples of things in nature to use as signs of Allah, the wide variety of seeds which produce so many different kinds of plants, or the way Allah made our planet Earth just the right distance from the sun. If the sun were closer, our planet would be too hot and if it were more distant it would be too cold. We need to be just the right distance for

Earth to be habitable. The Qur'an contains ninety–nine names for Allah. These can also be used to help the child understand who Allah is.

We need to check what children understand, because they can get confused. Young children are concrete thinkers. When told 'Paradise is at the feet of your mother', a child went over to her mother and stared at her mom's feet, puzzled. "Paradise is part of the floor?" she asked.

Allah made the wind and the sun but not the house. Mommy can explain how people built the house with materials Allah provided, like the trees for the wood and the copper for pipes and wires.

If we don't know the answer to a question, it is better to admit not knowing than to invent false stories. A parent can always check on the answer and supply it to the child later. Meanwhile, an invented lie contaminates the truth and can lead the child astray.

So if children are pure and sinless, why do bad things happen to them? How can Allah be the All Compassionate, the All Merciful if He allows little children to get badly hurt or sick?

Allah knows the world in which we live. There is illness and disease. There are disasters and just minor accidents when we hurt ourselves. And there are evils in the world and people who hate, who harm others.

No fatigue, nor disease, nor sorrow, nor sadness, nor hurt, nor distress happens to a Muslim, even if it were the prick he receives from a thorn, but that Allah wipes away some of his sins for that. (Bukhari)

Be moderate and stand firm in trouble that falls to the lot of a Muslim (as that) makes amends for some sins for him; even stumbling on the path or the prick of a thorn. (Muslim)

Since children have no sins to erase, Allah gives them rewards to compensate them for whatever harm they suffer. The rewards may come either in this life or the Hereafter.

The Prophet was asked, "Who are in Paradise?" He said, "Prophets are in Paradise, martyrs are in Paradise, infants are in Paradise, and children buried alive are in Paradise." (Abu Dawud) [The Arabs had a practice before Islam of burying unwanted daughters alive, a practice condemned strongly in Qur'an that Prophet Muhammad (s) was able to eliminate from the culture.]

We should tell our children of the difficulties of the prophets and the companions of Prophet Muhammad (s). Prophet Muhammad did not snap his fingers or wave a wand and make his world magically wonderful. He suffered multiple losses of his family. His parents, grandfather, and later all his children died before him except Fatima. He suffered famine and ridicule and people throwing rocks at him. He fought in battles.

With older children we can talk about how working through our problems makes us stronger and better people. We call on Allah and learn to trust Him to guide us through whatever we are facing. We become closer to Him.

We learn from the difficulties that happen to us and we are tested on how well we accept these difficulties and try to overcome them. A child who overcomes the difficulties of being blind in a world where others see, who works hard to read and learn and becomes a successful adult, will receive a great reward from Allah.

Allah, the Glorious and Exalted said, "When I afflict my slave in his two dear things (i.e., his eyes), and he endures patiently, I shall compensate him for them with Jannah [Paradise]." (Bukhari)

The one for whom Allah intends good, encounters difficulties to get it. (Bukhari)

Part of the test is also how the parents respond. If a child is born with disabilities, does the parent desert the child or fight to get the best help possible? The parent who reassures the child with love and supports the child's struggles in the world will be well rewarded for that.

We should never label a child as a bad kid even though we may have problems with him or her. The actions of a child may be bad. Labeling a child as bad is a way of saying the child can't be helped, that it is his or her nature to be bad. But the child is born in fitra, the pure being Allah

15

created. The recording angels will record our bad deeds, since we are adults, but they don't start recording any bad deeds for the child until puberty.

And indeed there are guardians over you, noble scribes, knowing whatever you do. (Qur'an 82:10-12)

"The pen has been lifted from three; for the sleeping person until he awakens, for the child until he becomes a young man and for the mentally insane until he regains sanity." (Tirmidhi)

There are three (kinds of people) whose actions are not recorded: a sleeper until he awakens, a child until he reaches puberty, and a mentally defective one until he comes to reason. (Abu Dawud)

In the Islamic understanding, the age of consciousness and reason, which occurs around puberty, marks the endpoint of childhood's freedom from responsibility. It is the consensus of the scholars from the four Sunni madhhabs [schools of Islamic legal philosophy] that this age is marked by the onset of menstruation for a girl and of wet dreams for a boy in a typical person. If these signs are late in coming, the scholars generally agree on the age of 15. Allah knows the time exactly for each. From that time on, a young person is considered responsible for his or her actions in front of Allah. In other words, he or she is considered an adult and accountable. We assume that the recording angel of each person starts to record the bad deeds then, and the prayers, fasting, and pilgrimages of Hajj and Umrah are counted as the actions of an adult. For those of limited mental capacity or suffering from mental illness, as seen in the hadith above, they may never be held accountable by Allah.

Modern psychology and research on the brain indicate that the brain is still developing and growing into the second decade of life, well beyond puberty. Theories about when a person should be held responsible for their actions are being discussed, moving older and older from what was commonly expected even fifty years ago. This, however, is a different study from what Muslim scholars have been considering. They have made their best estimates from their study of Qur'an and hadith and their understanding of their communities. We follow their guidelines knowing

16

that Allah knows much better than anyone when each person, at any age, will be held accountable and what weight to give each deed.

Young people have been doing adult work for centuries. Usama bin Zayd, companion of the Prophet, was given command of the Muslim army when he was only fourteen or fifteen. Young kings and princes in Europe have been given similar power. And we see children "grow up quickly" when their families are in difficulty due to divorce, a death in the family, or some other hardship, and children take jobs to help out or they care for younger brothers and sisters.

This consideration of entering adulthood is partly physical, with the development of the brain and the body, and partly related to how families and schools teach responsibility to their children. Many American children are being raised in controlled environments where safety is a priority and there is little financial need—so they spend their free time in safe, fun activities. They may be shielded from experiencing the consequences of their actions either because their activities are so sanitized there is little possibility of making mistakes or because adults want to be very encouraging and immediately clean up or erase any errors. Many young adults in their twenties might not seem to be capable of being responsible because they have never been allowed to learn how.

As Muslims, however, we need to assume that our children will be held accountable as adults when they mature into their teens. It's our job to give them responsibilities much earlier to train them so they can succeed.

An added incentive to encouraging children to do good deeds is because the recording angel does note the good deeds. A child learns the joy of participating with the family, being responsible, and earning reward from Allah when we encourage them to do good deeds.

Truly, Allah doesn't let the reward of the faithful ever become lost. (Qur'an 3:171)

"I'll never let the efforts of any of you who made an effort (on behalf of Allah) become lost, be he male or female, for you're equally from each other." (Qur'an 3:195)

Even a small child can learn to do something, like putting money into a collection box for charity or going to fetch Daddy's baseball glove from the closet. A smile can be a good deed as well as comforting Mama when she's sick by getting her a box of tissues. Helping fold the laundry and preparing the table for supper are good deeds and chores that prepare the child for adult responsibilities. Performing acts of worship also earn rewards.

Angels

So angels are recording our deeds, but what are angels? There are many stories about angels around in literature. Most of it is a lot of fantasy. We should stick to what is known from Qur'an and hadith rather than showing children pictures of lovely ladies with big wings.

We know that Allah created angels from light, which could include anything of the whole electromagnetic spectrum. We use this spectrum of energy today to send all kinds of signals and messages ourselves, but that doesn't mean we know what angels are at all. There are good records in Qur'an and hadith that angels sometimes take the form of humans to bring messages from Allah to people, like Prophet Muhammad and Mariam (Mary), mother of Prophet Esa (Jesus), (peace and blessings upon them all). But we don't expect that in our everyday lives. Angels join our prayers, our salah. They come close to us when we are doing good things and their presence helps evil stay away from us. They leave when we do bad things.

While many angels will stay away if we do something bad, there are always angels close to us to record our deeds. If scientists could discover this, they would probably look for ways to change the record. Allah has protected His angels from their probes.

Hopefully our children will find comfort in knowing about these beings. Some Muslims recite the two surahs of protection, Qur'an 113 and 114, with their children before bed to bring the angels close to them and give them a good night's rest. Aisha, the wife of Prophet Muhammad, was heard telling a member of her family to go to bed by saying, "Won't you let the recording angel rest?" (Muwatta) And we can explain to our children that when we give the Salam at the end of salah (formal prayer), we do it to both the right and left of us because it addresses the angels who are praying with us.

It is a duty for parents to educate themselves about what they teach their children so they can give them correct information. Young children, especially under the age of six or seven, have a hard time understanding the difference between fact and fiction. They need our help. We can't assume that they know when a fairy story isn't real. We need to state these things clearly to our children. Allah, His angels, jinn [defined below], Paradise, Hell, and the Day of Judgement are all real. Fairies, trolls, leprechauns, the Easter bunny, the tooth fairy, and such, these are all fantasy.

Don't confuse the truth with falsehood, nor conceal the truth knowingly. (Qur'an 2:42)

Jinn and Satan

There are a lot of stories in the Muslim community about jinn. "Don't throw hot water down the sink because jinn live in pipes and they will attack you," is an old wives' tale someone told a new convert to Islam. Some of the stories are fun entertainment but some can cause a lot of problems, particularly if adults get into the imaginative talk about someone being possessed by the jinn.

We don't need to talk about jinn until children start learning about them in Qur'an, unless a child heard something and asks about it. We should just stick to the facts that are in Qur'an and hadith and clarify for children when stories are invented about them. Some jinn are Muslim and others follow Satan, just like people do. Prophet Muhammad was sent as a messenger to them as well as to us.

Satan requires more thought and consideration. In the Islamic world view, the person is a creation of Allah. He or she has the choice between doing good, following the guidance of Allah, and doing bad, following the suggestions of Satan. We can always change who we listen to but it can take work to create the habit of screening out Satan and following Allah. We need to work on our inner strength, or will-power. We need to work on correctly identifying the source of our ideas and impulses. This doesn't happen overnight. It is a gradual process. Reciting Qur'an and praying help our brains construct positive pathways, filling our minds with what is good and giving less room or less opportunity to think what is bad. Working to think of good deeds to do also gives us less time to imagine bad things to do.

It is only recently that scientists have started realizing how much we are able to train our brains. But just as a speech therapist can work with a stroke victim and, with exercise and repetition, slowly rebuild the pathways of speech, so gradually with exercise and repetition we can direct our brains to healthy ideas, good speech, and following the will of Allah.

"Indeed Satan has an effect on the son of Adam, and the angel also has an effect. As for Satan, it is by threatening evil repercussions and rejecting the truth. As for the effect of the angel, it is by the promise of a good end and believing in the truth. Whoever finds that, let him know that it is from Allah, and let him praise Allah for it. Whoever finds the other then let him seek refuge with Allah from Satan [the outcast] then recite: **'Satan scares you with fears of poverty and tempts you to do shameful things, while Allah promises you pardon and grace. (2:268).** *'" (Tirmidhi)*

Some of the verses in Qur'an that tell us how Satan works include: 2:168, 17:53, 4:119-120.

No child is born without Satan's touching it at its birth whereupon it cries loudly from Satan's touching of it, except Mary and her son (Bukhari, Muslim)

Once when his wife Aisha was feeling jealous, the Prophet noticed it and asked her about it. He then said, "It was your satan who came to you," and she said, "Oh Messenger of Allah, is there a satan with me?" He said, "Yes." She said, "Is there a satan attached to everyone?" He said, "Yes." She said, "Oh Messenger of Allah, with you too?" He said, "Yes, but, my Lord has helped me against him so that I am safe from his mischief." (Muslim)

When a child has done something wrong, and knew it was wrong, we can start a little discussion with him or her. This is when we can help them identify that voice that encouraged them to action as the voice of something different from themselves, giving bad advice. Since it is not from themselves, they can argue with that voice and tell it "No!" or whatever they want to say. Show them how they have a choice whether to follow bad advice or to refuse it.

We teach them to use the surahs of taking refuge with Allah, Surah al-Falaq (113) and Surah an-Nas (114) as a means of protection against Satan and his works. We can explain to them that we say, "Audhu billahi min ash-shaytan ar-rajim" before we start reciting Qur'an or when we start doing anything else. We are asking for Allah's help to keep Satan away, so our efforts will be more successful.

There is also the voice inside the child that encourages good actions. "Mommy said not to touch the hot oven." "I need to brush my teeth." "Malik's cookie broke. I can give him some of mine." We help our child look for this voice and follow it. When we read Qur'an and pray, we are more likely to hear this voice and we will hear less of the bad voice.

We also need to talk to the child who is fearful that someone won't like them or that telling the truth might get them in trouble. These are some of the fears that Satan tries to exaggerate as he whispers to us. They are real fears and normal for us to have. But Satan can magnify them and try to stop us from doing what is right, or what is good. Praying to Allah for strength and guidance is one of the most useful things we can do. Talking about them with someone else can be helpful to strengthen us to manage our fears so they don't overwhelm us.

If any suggestion from Satan assails you, then seek Allah's protection, for He hears and knows (all things). Those who bring (Allah) to mind when an evil thought from Satan attacks them are reminded (of their allegiance to Allah) and suddenly they can see clearly again! (Qur'an 7:200)

We should not neglect to search for the possible tangible causes of any trouble our child is having. A child may be scared of something at school or disturbed from watching violent videos. On rare occasions, a child might have some mental illness or disability that we need to address. At the same time, we continually pray for Allah's protection from all harm, especially from Satan and his whispering, and ask earnestly for guidance and divine support. And when we ask Allah for help and guidance, He will never turn us away.

Paradise and Hell

Children grieve. They miss people or pets who leave them. We should talk about death, when the occasion brings it to us, even if we have trouble finding the words or feel inadequate. Simple words are fine. Hugs and holding hands may also be good communication without words.

Let children talk and question, even if they don't sound "properly respectful". Part of the grieving process is in these discussions and in sharing the loss together with those we love. Death, dying, and life beyond death are mentioned hundreds of times in Qur'an. From this emphasis on the subject, how can it possibly be one which we do not bring up and discuss with our children?

A man from among the Ansar came to him and greeted the Prophet (s) with Salam. Then he said, "Oh Messenger of Allah, which of the believers is best?" He said, 'He who has the best manners among them." He said, "Which of them is wisest?" He said, 'The one who remembers death the most and is best in preparing for it. Those are the wisest." (Ibn Majah)

There are descriptions of Paradise and Hell in both Qur'an and hadith. Some people, and particularly concrete thinkers, (and all children are concrete thinkers until about middle school age when they learn to think more abstractly) take all the details in these descriptions literally. Many adults consider them more abstractly, as the best way Allah and the prophet could describe the indescribable.

In today's world, these descriptions can be scary to a young child, if they understand them. For a child, the idea of gardens in Paradise may not sound very attractive. And many children today have little experience with fire unless their parents take them camping. It is probably best to keep discussion simple and on the level of the child's understanding. We might say something like, "Imagine the most wonderful house you could live in. What would that be like? Well Paradise is a far better than that."

A man came to the prophet (s) and asked if there would be camels in Paradise. The prophet answered, "If Allah admits you into Paradise, you will have in it whatever is desired by your soul and pleasing to your eye. (Tirmidhi)

Some people use the fear of death and Hell as a way to scare others to do good, or at least to do what they want done. While they are in Qur'an and hadith and a part of our religion, there needs to be a balance and moderation in our lives. We shouldn't give our children the idea that Allah is some mean being that watches our every move ready to pounce on us for any misstep. And we don't want them to assume Allah is like Santa Claus and never punishes anyone so Hell is just a joke. Yes, we fear Hell, but we hope for Paradise and work toward it. Allah gives us so much time to repent, to correct our mistakes, to pray for forgiveness. His mercy is far greater than His anger.

Allah says, (addressing the angels), "If My servant intends to do a bad deed, do not write it down unless he does it. If he does it, then write it down as it is. But if he refrains from doing it for My sake, then write it as a good deed. If he intends to do a good deed but does not do it, write a good deed (in his account), and if he does it, then write it for him as ten good deeds up to seven hundred times." (Bukhari, Muslim)

"All my followers will enter Paradise except those who refuse." They said, "Oh Allah's Messenger (s)! Who will refuse?" He said, "Whoever obeys me will enter Paradise, and whoever disobeys me is the one who refuses (to enter it)." (Bukhari)

Then Hell is understood as the final result of what people did for themselves. They refused Allah, in spite of many chances to improve.

A further argument against trying to scare children into behaving is that the recording angel doesn't record the bad deeds of children under the age of puberty, so any child who dies will be in Paradise. In a long hadith, the Prophet (s) spoke about a dream in which two heavenly guides showed him Hell and Paradise and their inhabitants. When he asked the guides about the meaning of the figures he had seen in both places, they replied in detail. Among their explanations was the following:

. . the tall man whom you saw in the Garden is Abraham, and as for the children who were around him, every child dies on fitra (the true religion)." At that, some Muslims said, "Oh Messenger of Allah, and the children of the idolaters?" The Messenger of Allah (s) said, "And the children of the idolaters (as well). (Bukhari)

2 – CHILDREN AND PARENTS

In the Islamic world view, the person is a member of a nuclear family, brothers and sisters and parents, that is part of an extended family, that is part of a neighborhood, part of a community, part of a social group that extends out around the world to include the sum total of all of the children, the descendants of Prophet Adam (s). We all have rights and obligations toward each other.

To focus on the parent-child relationship, the Qur'an has ordered us to be kind and respectful to our parents always and only disobey them if they try to turn us away from Islam. (Qur'an 17:23-24, 31:14, 29:8) It is in the basic fitra of the young child to look to parents for guidance, to look to them as the ideal parents and the ideal adults. This makes the parent's job relatively easy when children are young. Allah has set up a situation where children are ready to learn from their parents. But as children grow, seek out their own identity, and become adults, they will be making their own decisions. They will reevaluate their parents through their growing adult understanding and may have many differences of opinion with their parents. So Qur'an and hadith remind us of our continued debt to our parents for all of our lives.

We've made it an obligation upon every human being to show kindness to his parents. His mother carried him in discomfort and gave birth to him in pain. It took thirty months (for his mother) to carry him and finally wean him. Then, when he reaches the age of his full strength at forty years, he says, "Oh My Lord! Let me show my thanks to You for the favor You've given to me and to my parents, so that I can do the right thing as You would have me do. Be good to me in (the raising of) my own descendants. I have indeed turned myself to You and I am among those who submit (to You)." (Qur'an 46:15)

Prophet Muhammad called disrespect of parents one of the major sins.

The Prophet said three times, "Shall I inform you about the greatest of the major sins?" They said, "Yes, Messenger of Allah". He said, "To join others in worship with Allah and to be undutiful to parents." (Bukhari)

The greatest of the major sins are to make others partners with Allah and to murder a human being and to be undutiful to parents and (to speak) the false word," or, he said, "to bear false witness." (Bukhari)

Taking care of parents can be more important than fighting in a war.

"Oh Messenger of Allah! I want to go out and fight (for Allah) and I have come to ask your advice." He said, "Do you have a mother?" He said, "Yes." He said, "Then stay with her, for Paradise is beneath her feet." (An-Nasa'i, Baihaqi)

The mother is shown special consideration above the father by the Prophet.

Once a man came to the Prophet (s) and asked, "Who among people has most right to good treatment from me?" Tthe Prophet (s) said, "Your mother." He (the man) said, "Then who?" He said, "Your mother." He said, "Then who?" He said, "Your mother." He said, "Then who?" He said, "Then your father." (Bukhari, Muslim, Tirmidhi)

The father is not to be neglected though.

"The father is the middle door of Paradise (i.e. the best way to Paradise), so it is up to you whether you take advantage of it or not." (Ibn Majah)

This obligation is required even if our parents aren't Muslim.

Allah doesn't forbid you from being kind and fair to those who don't fight you because of your beliefs or drive you from your homes, for Allah loves the tolerant. (Qur'an 60:8)

Narrated Asma' (r), "My mother, who was a pagan, came with her father during the period of a peace pact between the Muslims and the Quraish. I went to seek the advice of the Prophet (s) saying, "My mother has arrived and she is hoping (for my favor)." The Prophet (s) said, "Yes, be good to your mother." (Bukhari)

Even after our parents have passed away, we have good things we can do for them.

A man came to the Prophet (s) and asked, *"Messenger of Allah, is there any kindness left that I can do for my parents after their death?" The Prophet (s) replied, "Yes. You can invoke blessings on them and forgiveness for them, carry out their final instructions after their death, join ties of relationship which are dependent on them, and honor their friends." (Abu Dawud)*

Parental Resolve

Children are a gift from Allah (swt) who knew best what child to give us. We should accept them and celebrate their birth and respect the nature of the child we received. Each baby is a surprise package. The child's personality, strengths and weaknesses are disclosed gradually over many months and many years. We will be able to downplay some aspects of a child's personality and encourage others. As the child matures, some aspects fade away and others develop. We will adapt ourselves to our child and the child will adapt to us as well. So we need to be ready to adapt our dreams for our children to account for the reality of who each child is.

David and his wife want their son to become a doctor. They have the money for their son's education and it is a much respected thing to be a doctor. Elijah, their son, likes math in school but hates biology. He is very squeamish and gets upset at the sight of blood. He loves building things. It started with Legos and just grew. Helping his father build a potting shed in the yard really sparked his interest. He draws well and particularly enjoys his engineering class in high school where they planned and drew robots and then built them. What's wrong with David and his wife modifying their dream to allow Elijah to become an engineer if he wants?

Faith always knew she wanted to have a daughter. She imagined how she would get her pretty things to wear and they would plan parties together.

27

A daughter would work beside her in the kitchen like she helped her mother. And someday she would get to plan a beautiful wedding for her daughter like her mother did for her. But Faith's daughter, Ayah, has Down Syndrome. That was not in her plans. However, Faith probably can do most of the things she wanted with her daughter anyway. Ayah will likely want to wear pretty clothes and help her mother with parties. She may have delays in her development compared to statistics for standard milestones. Faith needs to learn more about the syndrome and then see how it impacts her daughter, but she can still plan lots of enjoyable time doing things with her daughter.

Know that your property and your children are no more than a source of testing for you and that with Allah lies your most substantial reward. (Qur'an 8:28)

The believing man or woman continues to have affliction in person, property, and children so that he or she may meet Allah free from sin. (Tirmidhi)

The Messenger of Allah (s) delivered a speech to us. Meanwhile, (his little grandsons) al-Hasan and al-Husain arrived, stumbling and wearing red shirts. He came down from the pulpit, took them, and ascended it with them. Then he said, "Allah has said truly, **'Your wealth and your children may be a test for you..." (Qur'an 64:15).** *. Afterwards he resumed the speech. (Abu Dawud)*

One day the Prophet (s) came out carrying his grandchild, and he said, "You (i.e., children) become the means of stinginess, cowardice, ignorance, and foolishness. And you are also the fragrance of Allah." (Tirmidhi)

Children are a responsibility as well as a joy. We love them intensely and will make all kinds of sacrifices for them. They can bring out the worst in us. We worry over them. Our worry can make us stingy or act foolishly. But they can also bring out the best in our character as we try to be good role models for them, good teachers, good protectors, wise and strong. Allah, from His Bounty, gives children to us as He knows best. It is a test for us both to have children and to be unable to have children.

Allah has given us a high position over our children but He has also given us the very important job of caring for them and we will be held accountable for how we handle our job. This can seem overwhelming to many people but Allah has also told us in Qur'an:

Neither the mother nor the father should be treated unfairly on account of their child. (Qur'an 2:233)

This verse is especially important because it shows that Allah understands the complex issues that can come up with raising a child and the pressure other people can place on parents. This is a warning against too much social pressure. In-laws and the community should support parents. If a couple have a child with problems of some kind, it is unfair to blame the parents. They already have a burden greater than most parents. They need support in taking care of their child.

Another verse that is very important:

Allah will not burden any soul beyond what it can bear. (Qur'an 2:286)

Allah knows what kind of issues we will have with each child He gives us. And from this verse we know that we have it within us, even if we don't know how, to take care of this child and raise it. If Faith, in the example above, is overwhelmed with fear about her ability to raise a child with Down Syndrome, she needs to remember this verse. Allah will help her if she calls on Him. He knows she can do it, or He would not have given this child to her. She will learn and grow with this test and find joy with her child if she looks for it. Any parent with a child who has a disability or suffers from serious disease can take strength from this verse.

It's only due to Allah's mercy that you're gentle with the (believers in their time of stress), for if you were ever to be harsh with them they would scatter away from you. So overlook their shortcomings, pray for their forgiveness and seek their counsel on relevant issues. When you have come to a decision, then put your trust in Allah, for He loves those who trust in Him. (Qur'an 3:159)

This important verse of Qur'an summarizes the balance Prophet Muhammad made in teaching his companions. He chose the path of moderation. As Allah chose him to be the teacher of his community, to lead them to Islam, so Allah has chosen us to lead our children to Islam. We need to follow Prophet Muhammad and his resolve. He did ask for advice, from his wives and from a variety of other people around him. The companions came to him with many faults. He overlooked many errors and his lessons for them were not overwhelming or too difficult for them. And he was steadfast in preaching the message, through years of hardship and difficulty.

"Be moderate and adhere to moderation, for there is no one among you who will be saved by his deeds." They said, "Not even you, Oh Messenger of Allah?" He said, "Not even me. Unless Allah surrounds me with mercy and grace from Him." (Ibn Majah)

It is harder to be moderate than it is to be either too strict or too easy. When we look for the moderate path, we have to collect information from all directions and sort it, weigh it, and try to find that middle way. There are all sorts of decisions that parents need to make, both large and small.

In the parenting methods we will explore in this book, we need to always reflect on the general rule of moderation in all things. In one cultural community, it may be the norm for children to spend hours studying and parents can easily ask their children to spend an extra half hour of memorizing Qur'an each day. Their children and neighbors won't find such behavior unreasonable. Memorizing is considered a good skill and even non-Muslim children memorize poetry, songs, multiplication tables, and other things at school. But in some communities such school activities are considered poor teaching. Memorizing is thought to prevent children from being creative.

Muslim families may try to prevent outside influences from upsetting their goals, but children pick up the atmosphere of society quickly. If a child absorbs from others that memorizing is difficult and not important, parents may need to scale down their expectations to remain moderate within their environment. Rewards for memorization may need to be increased. It might be good for parents to try visiting families who do value memorization and create a club of children who share tips on how to memorize, work to coach each other and enter contests together.

Whether parents have a specific decision to make or they are planning a general family system, we have guidance from Qur'an to help us. We pray for guidance, take the best information we have, and consult with our children if they are old enough, and then we make the best decision we can, trusting in Allah for His help, either to make things work out right or to show us our errors and guide us to better decisions.

Respect

Part of the Islamic world view is the concept of adab, often translated as manners. It is a system of behavior that encourages polite tactful speech and actions toward other people no matter what we think of them. Before explaining the particular issue of respect due from children to their parents and from parents to their children, we first need an overview of the concept in Islam.

Contrary to what is often seen in society, we don't judge others as to whether they are worthy of respect or not. We are not the judges of anybody. That would be arrogant. It is part of the basic manners of a Muslim to be a good Muslim, for your soul, to act respectfully toward others, no matter who they are. So the imam and police officer get respect, but also any person who serves the Muslim or who crosses paths with him. Prophet Muhammad taught us by his example how we should treat our enemies with respect. They are all human beings placed on this earth by Allah and there is a certain level of respect for all of Allah's creation, no matter our personal feelings. It doesn't prevent us from seeking justice or protecting ourselves from them. But it guides us to do that in a manner that doesn't go beyond the limits set by Allah. When we go beyond His limits, we harm ourselves.

The concept of acting respectfully will come up over and over again throughout this book. Practicing the manners and morals of Islam improves our character and brings us closer to Allah. It doesn't prevent us from taking on problems that occur in life but shows us the best way to tackle them for outcomes that keep within the boundaries of successful life.

The order to respect parents is general. However, the specifics of what is respectful and what is not are culturally defined. It is reported that the Prophet's daughter, Fatima, would stand up if her father came into her home to see her, and he would kiss her on greeting her. We may have different ways of greeting each other today, but we should have some norms of behavior about what is respectful.

Modern society has many avenues of influence on children today, through videos and television, and social interactions with other children. Much of the message is of self-empowerment, following your own plans and doing what you want to do, no matter what your family is doing. Secular society has little use for family ties except when they are used to support the child in doing something. Friends are important and following the crowd of what everyone else is doing.

So modern secular society is "me" centered compared to the Islamic society where the parents are central. We re-center our family when we require our children to respect us. Allah has given parents a great responsibility to raise their children. With that responsibility comes the right to respect. We can't carry out our responsibilities properly if our children don't listen to us. A lot of parent burn-out occurs when parents feel obliged to sacrifice over and over for their children, but are expected to put up with thoughtless and rude behavior from those children all the time. Allah (swt) has given rights and obligations to parents and He has given children rights and obligations as well.

He is not one of us who has no affection for the young and no respect for the old, and who does not enjoin good and forbid wrong. (Ahmed)

Notice in this hadith that it's not a command for the adult to respect the child, but to have affection for them. While it is general that we should respect all people, the Prophet emphasized affection over respect for the child. Due to the difference in age and maturity and responsibility, the adult is above the child in the family or social hierarchy.

Haroon wants to go to the movies with his friends. His father has to respond with affection to him, wanting him to have fun with friends but also thinking of how late he would be out. Who are the friends and are they responsible? How can the father balance Haroon's need for fun with his siblings who also want to be chauffeured to different social activities? The father also needs to consider the family needs, of getting chores done like cleaning the house, as well as the need to have some family time activities and maybe the need for the whole family to visit a relative who is sick. Haroon's father has to consider a wide range of issues and be responsible for the whole family. So Haroon's request may be accepted or denied with gentleness and consideration by his father, and Haroon should respect his father's decision.

We respect our children's needs and take their wants into consideration. We respect the different natures that each child has, their talents and personalities when we are making decisions for them. We treat them with affection, remembering that Allah gave them to us as a gift. Children, on the other hand, are required to treat their parents with respect, and we need to teach this to them. Allah gave them these parents and trusted them to be responsible for the children. Children can disagree with their parents but they should do so in a respectful manner.

A man saw the Prophet (s) kissing his grandson Husain. He said, "I have ten children and I never kiss any of them." The Prophet (s) said, "The one who does not show tenderness will not be shown tenderness." (Abu Dawud)

Narrated Aisha (r), "A bedouin came to the Prophet (s) and said, "You (people) kiss the boys! We don't kiss them." The Prophet said, "I cannot put mercy in your heart after Allah has taken it away." (Bukhari)

When Fatimah, the Prophet's daughter, came to visit him, he got up for her, took her by the hand, kissed her and made her sit where he was sitting; and when he went to visit her, she got up for him, took him by the hand, kissed him, and made him sit where she was sitting. (Abu Dawud)

It is important to include here that many Muslims create such a warm environment of respect and everything is wonderful that they don't watch out for people behaving badly. Most child abuse is caused by relatives or adults close to the child, like teachers and neighbors, not by strangers. So we need to do frequent reality checks on what is going on. Parents should not be so busy acting respectful of others that they fail to protect their children from abusers. And children should not be pushed to be so respectful that they fear telling anyone if they are being abused. We need to listen to our children and observe their behavior.

While people often think of abuse as sexual or physical, the most common abuses are verbal and emotional. A person who calls a child a "useless idiot" is engaging in verbal abuse. Suppose a child doesn't do a chore or favor someone asked him to do, and that person whines, "So you don't care about me?" This is an example of emotional abuse. Someone who smiles with a condescending expression on their face while telling a girl she is useless at math and science, may pass unnoticed by the parent, but this is a common abuse used to discourage girls from these subjects. Children generally don't complain about these kinds of remarks but they can be very damaging to the child's self-confidence.

There are good programs available to train both children and adults about abuse issues. We should use them. Our hope is in Allah (swt) that our children will be safe, but we lock our house doors and teach our children to lock the door.

Treating Children Equitably

It is generally assumed that parents love their children dearly. However, personality clashes of all sorts can occur in parent-child relationships. A strict parent and a strong-willed child will usually have energetic disputes. A gentle, meek parent with a strong, active child may become totally dominated by the child. An energetic, action-oriented parent with a low-key, sensitive, introspective child will have conflicts as the child tries to duck away from the parent's energy. All this appears to be a matter of personal "chemistry," or the interrelatedness of the souls which Allah has created:

"Souls are like recruited troops: Those who have similar qualities are inclined to each other, but those who have dissimilar qualities, differ." (Bukhari)

Souls are troops collected together and those who were familiar with each other (in the Heaven from where these come) will have affinity with one

34

another (in the world) and those amongst them who opposed each other (in the Heaven) will also be divergent (in the world). (Muslim)

We don't like to admit that we have favorites among our children and we shouldn't. It is important to treat children with equity and not show our feelings. But these are natural feelings that even the prophets struggled with. Prophet Yacoub (s) was most attached to Yusuf (s) out of all of his sons. The boys seem to have known this. He knew his other sons were jealous of Yusuf and letting him go with them was a risk, but he risked it. Then he knew they had done away with Yusuf, but he managed along with them in spite of that and they continued their lives. He did his best to guide them in spite of their problems and misdeeds. We can understand from this story that even if we ourselves were to behave as well as the prophets, there will be problems among our children. But that doesn't mean we shouldn't try to balance our attention and efforts for each child.

Whenever you speak, speak justly, even if a near relative is concerned. (Qur'an 6:152)

All you who believe! Stand up firmly for justice as witnesses before Allah, and (be fair witnesses even if it's) against your own selves, your parents or your relatives, as well. (Qur'an 4:135)

There is a parallel to this in both the following Qur'anic verse and the hadith below relating to women:

Therefore, you should live with them in kindness and goodwill. If you become disenchanted with them, it may be that you are disliking something through which Allah will bring much good (for you). (Qur'an 4:19)

"A believer must not hate his wife; if he dislikes one of her characteristics he will be pleased with another". (Riyadh-us-Saleheen, Muslim)

We can do the same with our children. We can be so worried about one thing our child does that we miss all the other good things about him. When we pray to Allah to help us with a problem with this child, perhaps we should also think of something about the child we can thank Allah for.

35

This was very useful for Rubah when her son accused her of favoring his sister over him. Truthfully she did have a preference because her daughter was so much like herself and they enjoyed doing the same things together. But because she had worked on thinking of the good in her son, she could immediately hug him and tell him sincerely what she found special about him. And she can make an internal promise to herself to make an extra effort to balance between her children.

If a father is always comparing his middle son negatively to his older son, this does nothing except encourage his sons to fulfill the expectations of their father. The older son will try to be good and the middle son won't try and may even act out jealously against the oldest. Instead, the father can try picturing his middle son differently. In what kind of setting or career would someone like his son be an asset? The father thinks of his son as slow and plodding. Someone else could describe the boy as thoughtful and thorough. Reframed like that, maybe he could become a careful accountant? Or a good microbiologist, examining slides carefully for signs of disease?

He might try listening to other adults' impressions of the child and reflect on the difference between their impressions of him and his own. This will give him a clue about how realistic his own view is. If other adults and children seem to reflect the negative impression he has, then his child has a wider problem. Is it a problem with the child or with the environment? Is the environment strongly sports-centered and this boy isn't into sports? Or is the family very calm and relaxed while this boy gets easily excited and dramatic and causes an uproar? The group may be encouraging the negative image, and more work is needed to improve the environment for the child.

We have the child Allah sent us, in His great Wisdom. We should be grateful and work to make our expectations realistic for the character of each child.

Many children get labeled. This can happen at school as well as at home. Laila has three children, Yunis, her perfect student, Nur, the athletic one, and Siham, the bad-tempered one. Maybe Yunis has study anxiety, worried about not living up to his mom's expectations. He's really having trouble in physics. Is Laila pressuring him too much inadvertently? And why assume Nur can't be a good student as well as an athlete?

Siham does get mad easily and throws things. At six years old she still has temper tantrums. She reminds her mother of her uncle, her mother's little brother. Mom has continually said she's just like Uncle Anwar and refused to deal with Siham's behavior. No one could deal with Anwar when he was little either. Siham's teacher at school just views her as a problem student. She gets in trouble a lot and can't cooperate working with other children.

Each child is born with their own particular personality traits, but many things will change over time and with education from the parents and the social environment. While we need to respect how Allah has created each child, we also need to work with the child patiently and gently to see how they can grow and change. Many people have a tendency to get angry. But there are constructive ways to deal with anger so a person can control their behavior. Laila needs to stop comparing her daughter to her brother and learn ways to manage her daughter. It's not easy and may require outside help. Labeling children can be a way of giving up. It is a way of preventing children from changing and growing.

As Siham starts to improve at home, hopefully with a new school year she can start fresh and improve her behavior there. Talking about the problem with her teacher may help the school community accept the "new" Siham and not continue to label her as a problem.

Allah tests us for patience probably more than He tests us for anything else. We need to have patience with our children and give them the opportunity to surprise us as they grow and change.

It is important to remember Allah's saying that:

He's the One Who made you successors in the earth, and He's placed some of you in higher positions than others so He can test you with (the varying gifts) that He's given you. (Qur'an 6:165)

Each child has different gifts. Parents can encourage those gifts to flower and help the child control the weeds that come with those flowers. When we have been given more gifts than others, we will be tested for our pride and how we share our gifts with others. If we feel we have been given less than others, we will be tested on how we appreciate what we have been given and do as much as we can with them. Each person has the capacity to achieve Paradise. That should be our focus rather than who's better than who.

Often parents are tested by having children of one sex when they prefer the other. Today many people would still rather have sons than daughters, like the Arabs in the time of the Prophet (s) who saw no use in rearing a child who would be of no economic benefit to them and would leave to go to her husband's house once grown. But the Prophet (s) spoke of the great rewards promised to those who rear daughters, doing so purely for the pleasure of Allah and without hope of any economic benefit:

"Whoever raises two girls, then I and he will enter Paradise like these two." And he indicated with his two fingers. (Tirmidhi)

If anyone has a female child, and does not bury her alive, or slight her, or prefer his children (i.e. the male ones) to her, Allah will bring him into Paradise. (Abu Dawud) [The Arabs had a practice before Islam of burying unwanted daughters alive, a practice condemned strongly in Qur'an that Prophet Muhammad (s) was able to eliminate from the culture.]

A final issue concerning being equitable with our children concerns the provisions we give them and the gifts.

Nu'man ibn Bashir (r) reported, "My father took me to Allah's Messenger (s) and said, Allah's Messenger, bear witness that I have given such and such gift to Nu'man from my property." The Prophet (s) said, "Have you conferred upon all of your sons as you have conferred upon Nu'man?" He said, "No." Thereupon the Prophet said, "Call someone else besides me as a witness." And he further said, "Would it please you that they (your children) should all behave virtuously towards you?" He said, "Yes." The Prophet said, "Then don't do that, (don't give a gift to one to the exclusion of others)." (Muslim, Bukhari)

We don't have to always give our children the exact same thing or amount of money. The important word is equity as opposed to equality. If your daughter wants a new dress, check that her brother has reasonable clothes too, but don't buy him a dress. You didn't have the money to take the children to the zoo several years ago but now you do. So take your young son. And maybe you can pay for something special now for your older son, who missed out on the zoo years ago but isn't interested in going now. Zaid has three children, including one boy with serious autism who is unable to live alone or take care of himself. In his will, Zaid can leave up to a third of his wealth to take care of his autistic child. Then the rest of his wealth would be divided according to the standard Islamic divisions. For equity among our children, we use common sense.

Goal Setting from the Qur'an

What are our goals for our children? What guidance does the Qur'an give us?

Prophet Abraham (s) was a very important father whose two sons became prophets as well. Following guidance from Allah, he traveled to the valley where Mecca (Makkah) is today and settled his wife Hajar there with his little son Ismael. He left them there and prayed for them, that they would establish prayer there and be supported by people in the area. He trusted that Allah would provide for them while he was gone, taking his sheep elsewhere in the search for grazing for them. He thanked Allah for giving him children, even though he was getting old and might worry about what would happen to them if he should die while they were small. He prayed for his children and his descendants, that they would all be people of prayer. (Qur'an 14:35-41, 2:128)

The prophets did not ask for worldly success for themselves and their descendants. Instead they asked, first, that Allah would accept their service, and then, that they and their descendants might be worthy servants, worshipping their Lord according to the rites of worship which He had revealed to them. Prophets are our examples for how to live. Shouldn't we make these our goals also?

Abraham's grandson Jacob (Yakub) was also a prophet and prayed:

"My children, Allah has chosen this way of life for you, so don't leave this (earthly) life unless you're surrendered (to Allah)." (Qur'an 2:132)

His focused advice and goal for his children was that they follow Allah (swt). And when his sons came to ask his forgiveness for having treated their brother Joseph (Yusef) so badly he said:

"I shall ask forgiveness for you from my Lord. Truly, He is the Most Forgiving, Most Merciful" (Qur'an 12:98).

Jacob is an example for us of a man who knew his sons had done something horrible to their brother. But he continued to live among them and guide them as best he could. He had to be patient for many years before he was reunited with his son Joseph. Despite all his grief he remained constant in serving Allah (swt).

Prophet Zachariah (s) was childless for many years, like Prophet Abraham. His prayer is preserved in Qur'an:

"My Lord, give me a pure and virtuous descendant of my own, for You hear all requests." (Qur'an 3:38).

And Allah gave him a son who grew to be a prophet as well, John, (Yahya).

So the prophets in Qur'an generally desire for their children that they grow up to be people of prayer who follow Allah. They aren't shown praying for power or good health. Maybe the prophets prayed for other things for their children, but the Qur'an doesn't show us that. This is the example Allah wants us to follow.

Another well-known father mentioned in the Qur'an is not a prophet but the wise man Luqman, for whom a surah of the Qur'an (Surah 31) is named. Luqman gives a little more specific advice than the prophets. Along with encouraging his son to follow Allah, he also tells his son to be patient with whatever happens to him and not be arrogant. He tells him to act with moderation and speak softly as well. His advice is simply stated and gives guidance to all of us. (Qur'an 31:13, 17-19)

40

Prophet Noah (Nuh) (s) was sent with a message from Allah (swt) to all of his people. How difficult it must have been for him to discover one of his own sons was among those who refused to listen to him. We can do our best and pray for our children, and things may not work out as we would want. It's very hard. His son refused to join the boat with his family and be safe, and he was lost with so many others in the flood. And Allah told Noah there were other things his son had done wrong as well that Noah had been unaware of. In spite of his pain, Noah didn't turn away from Allah. He accepted and continued to listen to Allah. (Qur'an 11:42-47)

The Qur'an also contains two general prayers for parents:

"Our Lord! Grant us spouses and children who will be a comfort to our eyes, and make us leaders in righteousness." (Qur'an 25:74),

"If you grant us a perfect and healthy child, we promise that we'll be thankful." (Qur'an 7:189),

Here Allah shows us that we can ask for healthy beautiful children who bring us comfort, as well as for children who will be pious and good Muslims. He knows our desires and our dreams.

Three prayers are answered, without doubt: that of a parent, that of a traveler, and that of one who has been wronged. (Abu Dawud)

We all pray for our children, and lift up our hands to Allah in supplication, knowing from hadith in Tirmidhi that He is shy to turn them away empty.

The Messenger of Allah said: "There is none who utters a supplication, except that Allah gives him what he asked, or prevents evil from him that is equal to it – as long as he does not supplicate for something evil, or the cutting of ties of the womb." (Tirmidhi)

Gentleness from Hadith

Allah is gentle and He loves gentleness. He rewards for gentleness what is not granted for harshness and He does not reward anything else like it. (Muslim)

There are many hadith of Prophet Muhammad (s) interacting with children. In these hadith we see continually how patient and caring he was. He could tease them lightly and was always thoughtful with them. A few of these hadith are included here:

Once the Messenger of Allah (s) kissed his grandson al-Hasan while a companion named al-Aqra (r) was sitting beside him. At that, al-Aqra (r) said, "I have ten children and l have never kissed any of them." The Messenger of Allah (s) glanced at him and said, "The one who is not merciful will not be shown mercy." (Bukhari).

Narrated Anas ibn Malik: "I served the Prophet (Muhammad) at Medina for ten years (when) I was a boy. Not everything I did was (to his liking), but he never (rebuked me even gently), nor did he say to me, 'Why did you do this?' or 'Why did you not do that?'" (Abu Dawud, Muslim, Bukhari)

The Prophet (s) got some ornaments presented by Negus [the Abyssinian king] as a gift to him. They contained a gold ring with an Abyssinian stone. The Messenger of Allah (s) turning his attention from it, took it by means of a stick or his finger, and then called his granddaughter Umamah, the child of Abul'As and Zaynab, and said, "Wear it, my dear daughter." (Abu Dawud).

Abdullah ibn Jafar, the Prophet's cousin, reported that when the Messenger of Allah (s) came back from a journey, the children of his family would welcome him. Once, when he came riding into Madinah from a journey, the young Abdullah was the first to go to him, and the Prophet (s) pulled the boy up to sit in front of him. Then came one of the two sons of Fatimah, and the Prophet (s) pulled him up to sit behind him, and that was how the three entered Madinah, riding on a mount. (Muslim)

Narrated Ibn 'Abbas: the Messenger of Allah (s) was carrying Al-Hasan bin 'Ali upon his shoulder, so a man said, "What an excellent mount you are riding, Oh child." So the Prophet (s) said, "And what an excellent rider he is." (Tirmidhi).

The servant of the Prophet, Anas bin Malik (r) said, I have never seen anyone kinder to his family than the Messenger of Allah (s). (His infant

42

son) Ibrahim was sent to the suburb of Madinah for nursing. He used to go there and we would accompany him. He entered the house (of the wet nurse), and it was filled with smoke, since the foster-father was a blacksmith. He took him (Ibrahim) and kissed him, and then came back. (Muslim)

Anas (r) also described the death of Ibrahim (r) at the age of eighteen months: *We went with the Messenger of Allah (s) to the blacksmith, Abu Sayf, who was the husband of Ibrahim's wet nurse. The Messenger of Allah (s) took Ibrahim and kissed him and sniffed him. Then after that we came in to him, and at that time Ibrahim was breathing his last, and the eyes of the Messenger of Allah (s) began to shed tears. At that, Abdur Rahman ibn Awf said, "Even you, Oh Messenger of Allah?" He said, "Oh Ibn Awf, this is mercy." Then he wept more and said, "Surely the eyes shed tears and the heart is grieved, but we do not say except what is pleasing to our Lord, and we are grieved by your parting, Ibrahim."* (Bukhari)

This is the example of Prophet Muhammad with children.

"Verily, kindness is not found in anything except that it beautifies it, and it is not removed from anything except that it disgraces it." (Muslim)

Financial Responsibility

We learn a great deal about the Islamic world view if we look at advice in Qur'an and hadith about how money should be spent. There is never an endless supply of money and we all need to make decisions about how we spend. How much for charity? How much for entertainment? How much for food and clothes? Can we afford children? We look to our religion for answers.

Do not kill your children for fear of poverty, as We provide resources for you and for them. (Qur'an 6:151, 17:31 is similar)

This verse should be understood in a large way. If the parents do not have resources, their families can be called in to help. If help is needed beyond that there is the local community. If there is some widespread famine or disaster in the community, then the nation or the world is responsible for helping. There are resources in the world to provide for all children. Allah is the All Bountiful and Most Generous.

This verse encourages us to welcome each child. We will be able to manage. Allah will provide! And He has given us a lot of guidance on how to spend what He has given us.

(Righteousness) is spending of your wealth, for love of Him on relatives, orphans, the poor, travelers, and on those who ask (for help). (Qur'an 2:177)

Two verses of the Qur'an specifically discuss issues of family obligations. The first verse generally gives the economic support of women to the men of their families. Allah created the family with balanced roles between men and women. Women have the physical burden of pregnancy and nursing. Men have the burden of providing financially for the family.

Men are responsible for the welfare of women since Allah has given some (of you) more wherewithal than others, and because they must spend of their wealth (to maintain the family). (Qur'an 4:34)

When Allah (swt) gives men a "degree" over women (Qur'an 2:228), it is largely in reference to this financial responsibility, since he is responsible for the whole family's welfare and for the bills.

Mothers should nurse their children for two full years. This (time period) is for the one who can complete this term. (During this time, the father,) the one to whom the child was born, must support (the expenses of the child) according to his means, though no one will be forced to do more than he is able. Neither the mother nor the father should be treated unfairly on account of their child. This also applies to whoever must assume responsibility (in the event of the father's death). ... (Qur'an 2:233)

In addition to understanding the financial obligation of the father from this verse, there is the important issue of equity described here. Both for the financial responsibility of the father and the nursing responsibility for the mother, Allah acknowledges that people can have difficulty fulfilling these goals if they were too strictly enforced. Some mothers don't have milk and some fathers don't have jobs.

Notice that it doesn't say in the event of the father's death, the mother is responsible for the financial support of the child. The first place to look for that support is to the man's father and brothers, the child's paternal relatives. The continuation of this verse allows the parents to decide to have another woman nurse the child, with the clarification that the decision be agreed upon by both parents and that the nursing mother be paid properly for her service.

When a woman's health is at risk from her pregnancy, or during delivery, scholars have said this verse requires the doctor or midwife to save the mother's life if they have to make a choice between her or her baby. Her health comes first. It's also from this verse that scholars push divorced parents to come to a mutual balanced agreement for the care of their children.

Many hadith encourage spending on our family and creating a good balance between giving in charity and helping family. Family in this context is not just the father, mother, and kids. Extended family is included, grandparents, aunts and uncles, and anyone who is in need in the family. Some of this advice:

Of the dinar you spend in Allah's path or to set free a slave or as a charity given to a needy person or to support your family, the one yielding the greatest reward is that which you spend on your family. (Muslim)

When a Muslim spends on his family seeking reward for it from Allah, it counts for him as sadaqah. (Bukhari, Muslim)

A man came to the Prophet (s) and said, "Messenger of Allah, I have property and children, and my father asks for my property." He replied, "You and your property belong to your father; your children come from the pleasantest of what you earn; so enjoy from the earning of your children." (Abu Dawud).

This last hadith doesn't mean there is no distinction between a man's money and his father's money. A son succeeds in life in part because of his parents, and he should share with them. It is very sad to see a successful doctor with his family in a big expensive house, while his parents work hard to pay the rent on a small apartment in a poor neighborhood. The doctor can spend well on himself and his children and ignore the difficulties of his parents? No. The Prophet recognized the right of the parents to ask for their sons to help them. Also people recognize from this that the care of elderly parents is an obligation for the children, particularly the sons. Allah has been generous with the son and he should be generous with his family.

The Prophet (s) used to spend from his property on his family, and give the rest as sadaqah. (Abu Dawud)

The upper hand (the giver) is better than the lower hand (the recipient). One should start giving first to his dependents, and the best charity is what is given by a person from what is left after his expenses. And the one who refrains from asking others for help, Allah will give to him and save him from asking others, and the one who is satisfied with what Allah has given him, Allah will make him self-sufficient. (Bukhari)

So people aren't encouraged to be pushy in asking for help. But people are encouraged to look for those around them who might be in need and help them even if they don't ask.

The advice of the Prophet to one woman is interesting. He told her she didn't need her husband's permission to take from him to provide for herself and their children, though he cautioned her to be reasonable and not take more than necessary.

Hind bint Utbah said, "Oh Messenger of Allah, Abu Sufyan (her husband) is a miser and he does not give me what is sufficient for me and my children. Can I take from his property without his knowledge?" The Prophet (s) said, "Take what is sufficient for you and your children, and the amount should be just and reasonable." (Bukhari)

In giving this advice, the Prophet knew this couple and had an expectation of how Abu Sufyan would respond. Some men might respond very violently and the wife could be putting herself at serious risk to do this. Anyone giving advice needs to be careful about the situation. When a

46

man refuses to support his wife and children, he is giving his wife solid grounds for divorce. He is not doing his duty before Allah.

We should help family members even when we are upset with them. Some relatives can be very difficult people. Abu Bakr (r) had one such relative. A long hadith in Bukhari tells the story of how one of his relatives was a major accuser against Aisha (r), Abu Bakr's daughter and wife of Prophet Muhammad (s). She was accused of having an affair with a young man. Allah (swt) revealed the truth and cleared her name. Abu Bakr was very upset and swore he would stop giving any financial help to his relative, help that his relative depended on. Then this verse was revealed:

Don't let those who've been endowed (with great wealth and status) among you swear that they're no longer going to help their relatives, the needy or those who've migrated in the cause of Allah (simply because those people might have behaved poorly). Forgive them, and overlook (their faults). Don't you want Allah to forgive you, too? Allah is forgiving and merciful! (Qur'an 24:22)

And Abu Bakr responded quickly to this revelation and started supporting his relative again. The next verse after this in the Qur'an does promise Allah's punishment for those who slander innocent women. We shouldn't worry about helping our relatives who are in need, even if they do bad things. Allah will handle whatever bad they do and we are free of the burden of having to judge them.

A woman has no requirement to spend on her family. Any money she earns is hers. If she spends on her family, this is sadaqah from her.

Um Salama asked the Prophet (s), "Oh Messenger of Allah, shall I be rewarded if I spend to provide for Abu Salama's sons, when they are my sons as well?" The Prophet (s) replied, "Spend on them, and you will get a reward for what you spend on them." (Bukhari)

Zaynab, the wife of Abdullah ibn Masud, used to provide for Abdullah and those orphans who were under her protection. She asked the Prophet (s) whether it was permissible for her to spend from her zakah for them. The

Prophet (s) said, "Yes, and she will receive a double reward: one for helping relatives and the other for giving zakah." (Bukhari)

So we have good examples of women supporting their families financially during the time of the Prophet. Women who help their families will be well rewarded by Allah. But the respect for women in the Muslim community does not rest on their successful careers in the workplace. They are respected for their ability to create a comfortable home for the family. There is a verse in Qur'an that tells the wives of Prophet Muhammad, "Stay quietly in your homes," (Qur'an 33:33) in a section of advice for them and they have been considered the role models for all Muslim women.

When people were nomads, they might live in tents and travel far and wide for their herds. But the extended families traveled together. Everyone had things to do in their camps. Cousins played together as their mothers and aunts managed the cooking and home life while their fathers managed the herds. In towns and villages, Muslims built houses that were rather closed to the outside world, but open and light inside with courtyards, fountains and gardens. This was the world of the women and children of the family, a protected place of comfort. A widow, divorcee, or other woman in financial distress was supported by the men of her extended family or by help from zakah or sadaqah, so there was no economic necessity for a woman to leave the home to work outside.

Traditional society also didn't have factories dominating towns. Workshops for making things were attached to people's homes. Both men and women worked in and around their homes and farms, in kitchens preserving food, in gardens and fields, spinning and weaving, doing metal crafts and sewing. And there were no machines to do the work so preparing food and making clothes was a long process. Staying home didn't imply not working, but a safer environment for a woman close to those she loves and cares for. For fishermen and men who traveled for a living, like soldiers and merchants, the women were the bedrock of their families, holding the home together until the men's return. But these homes were also embedded in neighborhoods, stable places where people knew each other and lived nearby for generations. These networks of people created solid communities with traditions and roots that helped members overcome life's difficulties.

48

Today life is very different. Everyone is focused on careers for both men and women. The economic situation and living conditions are very different. The network of men in the family who can and will help out financially when a woman needs it—that network is generally nonexistent. Most women don't work for fun but for real financial need.

And in many places, if a woman stayed home to care for her children, she would be alone, isolated, and her children would have no playmates. All the other mothers work and their kids are in daycares. Family members usually live a distance away, not in the home or just across the street. Neighborhoods are created by housing developers but not by networks of people who know each other and feel a sense of community. People move frequently. Much of life has moved on-line, further separating live interactions with people.

So we need to think carefully about the real situation of families and not insist on a lifestyle that may no longer be realistic. Just requiring a woman to stay home with her children does not ensure a good outcome for either the children or the mother if the society and the economic reality of the time do not support the mother. But the environment of home for young children with adult caretakers who really care about the child is something we should really strive to create if possible.

The situations today are varied and complex and there is no one-size-fits-all response. An additional aspect with long life spans today, is that the child-raising years are an increasingly smaller part of the lives of women and men and we need to adjust our plans for that. We don't marry and raise kids, then retire and rest for a few years before illness and death. People must plan to live in reasonable health until their eighties today. They need financial support for all of those years so planning careers and investing in them is very important for both men and women. Divorce plays a role in planning. Some people may be married for 60 years together, but many couples will separate over the years. Since jobs come and go over time in today's economy, women need to prepare themselves to be able to support their family at least some time during their lives, even if, when they marry, everything looks economically positive for them to be able to stay home rather than work.

Couples need to discuss these issues seriously, probably before marriage. What are their expectations? Could one of them work from home? One family found that the father could work from home and manage the childcare most of the time until the mother returned from work. For the few years of preschool, they put their children in a part time preschool program to provide their children with more social activities than the father could manage around his workload. Then when the children were older and in school, he made time in the afternoon for them when they came home. The mother spent more time with the children in the evenings and on weekends, when the father put in more work time. The parents pooled their income and discussed together how to manage their joint expenses and provide in a balanced way for both of their wants and needs. So they created a safe comfortable environment for raising their children, even if it was very different from the traditional model.

Considering the high status given to the mother in Islam, higher than the father's, and second only to Allah in deserving respect, it is easy to see why Muslim women usually desire children and why many of them have been happy to stay home and care for them in the past.

Each one of you is a guardian and is responsible for what is in his custody. The ruler is a guardian of his subjects and is responsible for them. A husband is a guardian of his family and is responsible for it. A woman is a guardian of her husband's house and is responsible for it. And a servant is a guardian of his master's property and is responsible for it. (Bukhari)

Being a guardian does not mean being a servant to or a prisoner of. It does mean taking oversight of the home, and the children and any servants there.

Nannies or relatives can substitute for the mother, either temporarily or over the long term. The verse (Qur'an 2:233) above establishes the important role of the mother in nursing her child. Nursing is an extension of the pregnancy. Extending from there, mothers have usually been the primary caregiver of the young child and most women enjoy that role. But the verse continues and describes employing a woman to nurse the baby, and the importance of the parents coming to agreement on how to take care of the child.

The mother of Prophet Muhammad (s) did not nurse him, or even see him every day. Shortly after he was born, he was given to a Bedouin woman, Halimah al-Sa'diyah. Women who lived in towns did this if they could afford it, because infant mortality rates were high and people knew that a child was usually healthier living out in the desert, away from the town. Prophet Muhammad lived with Halimah and her family traveling out in the desert. She nursed him and raised him with her own children.

Women who did this were called milk-mothers (wet-nurses) and they have high status in Islam for the children they nurse. Their children are milk-siblings and can't marry children nursed by their mother. They are considered like half-brothers or sisters. Muhammad always treated Halimah with great respect when he met her later in life. The Prophet's son Ibrahim was also placed with a milk-mother and probably his other children as well. However, from the Qur'anic wording, "It is no sin for you" if a wet nurse is used, and from the mention of mother's nursing first, scholars understand that the better way is for a mother to nurse her child if possible.

We should think about the importance Allah gives to the milk-mother when we think of who should take care of our children when they are little. A strong bond can form between a child and his or her nanny or foster mother, or daycare worker that is very important for the emotional development of the child. Yet in many places, people drop their children off at daycares without any clear idea of who is taking care of their child.

The value to the child of not needing to wake at 6 am, dress and rush off to a daycare, so parents can get to their jobs, is something we can't calculate in money. The quality of time playing around the house near Mom or Dad is different from the time spent in a classroom playing under the observation of a childcare worker. But we can't calculate that either. There is stability and security in having long term relationships with people who care about the child and aren't just thinking about their paycheck. And there is security for the parents, knowing the moral and social environment is of their making, and not one instituted by the State and the secular society that has been created to ensure that all children, from every background, get a standardized basic level of care.

Wherever possible we should select caretakers for our children carefully and support a good bond between the woman and our child. We should respect this relationship of our child even after the child has moved on to school age. It isn't as high a relationship as a milk-mother but it can be very important. In the first 6 years of life a child learns his or her identity, nationality, gender, and forms basic assumptions about how the world works. Is life a struggle? Do people pay attention to me and respond to my needs? Is the world a warm and loving place? Can I take care of my basic needs to feed myself, to dress and wash myself or do I need constant attention? Do I share with others or do I need to protect my stuff all the time? A basic world view is formed in these early years that is very difficult to change later.

Women today can feel guilty for staying home, worrying about future career options. They can feel guilty for going to work and leaving their children to others. But Allah is merciful and understands our situations better than we understand them ourselves. The recording angels record our intentions as well as our deeds and Allah knows our efforts and love for our children. If we pray and ask for guidance, and then do our best according to our understanding of our situation, Allah will help us to a good outcome for our families and protect us from harm if Allah wills.

Well how about the father? Remember back in our description of the traditional ideal life for a Muslim family, the father usually worked out of his home. If he was a farmer, people can picture that easily. But shops in the market usually had family living quarters upstairs or in the back. Craftsmen set up their workshops in a room of their houses. Fishermen and traveling merchants, or herders might be out away for months at a time, as were soldiers, but many fathers were close and available for their children. Children watched their fathers' work and often helped out. Fathers were there to lead family prayers or to guide the children across the street to the local mosque.

Today's fathers can work from home sometimes, particularly if they are working on-line. But much work requires fathers to be absent, off in an office or other place of business, often with a long commute time. Some fathers are gone so much, they don't see their children except on the weekends. In situations of divorce, some fathers might see their children even less. It is then the responsibility of the mother or other guardians to remind the children of their father in a positive way, even if their relationship with him is strained. In making career choices, both mothers and fathers need to consider how to balance time between career and family.

Scientists of child development have observed that children who have a strong father figure in their lives tend to do better in establishing themselves as adults. Boys need that vision of a man as a role model to challenge themselves and guide them to become men. Girls need that relationship with their father to guide themselves in choosing a husband or in managing around men in the workplace.

And children need more than just an image of their father. They need a father active in their lives as much as possible. In today's modern world, parents need to work together to share parenting time with their children. Dad can give the kids baths and get them to bed when his schedule allows. He can cook and take a child shopping for shoes. And he definitely needs time to play games with them or maybe volunteer to coach their sports team. They need to hear his advice and laugh at his jokes.

Narrated Al-Aswad, "I asked Aisha what did the Prophet (s) do at home. She replied. "He used to keep himself busy serving his family and when it was time for the prayer, he would get up for prayer."" (Bukhari)

There are certainly children who have no fathers, or who grow up with little contact with them. Prophet Muhammad was one such child. But he had his grandfather and uncle for role models.

Most women and men will find great joy and satisfaction in their roles as parents, and some people don't realize this joy until they try it. So, it is socially normal to encourage people in this direction. But there will always be some people for whom marriage and/or children, isn't desired. So though we should encourage people to marry and have children, we shouldn't push too hard. If Allah has given someone children and they don't feel up to the role of parent, we need to help out, for the sake of both the parent and the children.

Excess spending

The world view of Islam concerning money extends beyond who works in the family and how we organize childcare. Today it is common for parents to buy too many toys and games or worry because they can't afford to. A few well-chosen toys, suitable to the level and interest of the child, can be a source of education and entertainment. However, a common situation for young children is a room full of half-broken, unused toys, and a child who whines for more and fights with others over possession of the unused piles. With older children it is often the overuse of video games and TV for entertainment. How many game systems does a child need? And each has multiple games.

Concerning this, Allah says:

All you who believe! Don't forbid the good things that Allah has allowed for you. Just don't overindulge (in lawful things), for Allah has no love for the overindulgent. (Qur'an 5:87)

Now ask them, "Who has forbidden the exquisite (gifts) of Allah, which He has made available to His servants, and (who has forbidden) the wholesome (things He has) provided?" (Qur'an 7:32)

Along these lines, having a piece of candy as a special treat now and then is a pleasant experience for a child. But if she is given as much candy as she wants every day, she will quickly lose her enjoyment of it; candy will become just another routine food. And she won't be eating a healthy diet. Excess is not good for us.

While there are many families that struggle to get the basic necessities of life, we also have large numbers of families who have been blessed with wealth. Due to the design of neighborhood construction in many towns and cities, the poor and wealthy often live apart. In wealthy neighborhoods, hearing what the neighbors just bought encourages people to buy more. And poor families, imagining wealthier families from a distance, often feel pressure to buy more for their children than they can afford, in fear that their children will be penalized in life for missing out on the latest technology games.

Islam is a religion of moderation in all things. We will be asked on the Day of Judgement about how we spent our money. The recipe is simple, boring perhaps, and difficult to follow. Spend some, save some, and give some to the poor. How much for each category? It varies for each family. It varies with different cultural expectations in different places. If we thank Allah daily for all He has provided us, pray to Him for guidance, and reflect regularly on how we are dividing up our money, Insha Allah we will find a reasonable balance that is healthy for our family.

The Education of Children

There are only a few hadith that clearly address parents about educating their children.

A father gives his child nothing better than a good education. (Tirmidhi and Baihaqi)

And in a time when baby girls were buried alive, the Prophet placed special emphasis on the reward for rearing and educating girls, saying:

"The one who brings up two girls properly until they grow up, he and I would come (close together like this) on the Day of Resurrection," and he interlaced his fingers. (Muslim)

The one who cares for three daughters, educates them, helps them marry, and does good for them, for him is Paradise. (Abu Dawud)

There is a wealth of material in Qur'an itself as well as hadith that encourages the believers to study the world and learn how Allah created it. And to be a good Muslim requires education. We need to be able to recite Qur'an and learn the prayers. We need to determine the times of prayers and of starting and breaking fasting days. The first word revealed of Qur'an was the word ordering "Read!"

Since education often involves paying for lessons, this is part of the father's responsibility to provide for his children. Mothers can certainly be involved as well. Both men and the women around the Prophet were actively involved in asking questions and trying to learn more about the religion. Women came to the Prophet and asked him to provide them with a specific time just to teach them. The men had been crowding around the Prophet when he taught in the mosque so that the women had felt crowded out. They asked for their own time and he arranged regular time for classes just for them. People sent their older children to learn from the Prophet's wife Aisha and from other companions who welcomed the chance to teach. Small schools evolved around different people who were known for their religious knowledge. With time these developed into formal education systems usually attached to mosques.

Adoption and Foster Care

Raising children is a very important activity and Allah has designed safety nets to protect children when problems arise. Children are not just the responsibility of parents. Outside of this circle is the circle of the larger family. And outside of this circle is the Muslim community. When children's needs cannot be properly met by parents, for whatever serious reason, the larger family becomes responsible, the grandparents and aunts and uncles, wherever there are resources. If this net should fail, in times of economic downturns, war, famine, disease, natural disaster, or for any other reason, the greater community has the responsibility to step in and take care of the child. Orphanages may be stop-gap solutions in some times and places, institutions for short term care of children while other arrangements are prepared, but for long term care the best place for a child is in a home with adults who volunteer to provide the love and care of parents for the child.

The first concern of the extended family or community, when called in over concern for a child, is to see if there are ways to support the child's family so that the child can stay with them. The biggest need is usually financial assistance. So charity funds are a big help. Sometimes a child needs to live in another home. Then foster care becomes important.

An example of foster care comes from the life of the Prophet. When the Prophet's uncle Abu Talib was in financial difficulties. Muhammad (s) and his uncle Abbas each took responsibility for one of Abu Talib's younger sons, and Ali joined the Prophet's household. So the Prophet was a foster parent for his cousin. Ali could have remained in his father's house, but a decision was made for him to move in with the Prophet, where he could be mentored as well as financially supported.

Mentorship and fostering are both important concerns in considering the best circumstances for a growing child. Where extended family is not available, it is up to the whole Muslim community to provide foster care until the family can resume care. If the family will not be able to resume care, then an adoption placement should be sought.

Of special consideration is the child who is an orphan. In Arabic, there are different words to describe a child whose mother has died from a child whose father has died. Each denotes a tragedy for the child, but it is recognized that each tragedy has different consequences.

A child whose mother has died is not considered a "yateem", translated as "orphan" in English, because the child has a father to support him or her financially, so it is expected the child will not be without food or clothing. Another word is used to describe this child. When the mother has died, it has traditionally been considered normal that the women of her family raise the child until adolescence, when the child returns to the father's household. But every circumstance is different and this foster care can be delegated in whatever way works best for the child and the family. Even if the father is caring for the children, it is encouraged that any women in the child's family assist him.

It is the child whose father has died who is called an "orphan", using the term "yateem" from the Qur'an, and the verses seek to encourage people to care for these children.

And how can you understand what the steep road is? It is the freeing of a slave or the feeding on a hungry day of orphaned relatives or of the poor person lying in the dust. (Qur'an 90:12-15)

Didn't He find you [Muhammad] an orphan and shelter you? Didn't He find you lost and show you the way? Didn't He find you in need and make you independent? Therefore, don't be mean to the orphan nor scoff at the requests (of the poor) and continue to declare (the mercy) and blessings of your Lord. (Qur'an 93:6-9)

When children are left orphaned, Muslims first make a search among near relatives to find someone to financially provide for them. This does not intrude on the position of the child's mother if she is present. This guardian, of sorts, can provide for the child while the child continues to live with the mother, who should be consulted and involved in any decisions made about the child. She may be appointed to this position herself and in today's world, where women often have good educations and careers, this is usually the best decision.

The prophet and his companions married widows to take care of them and their children. Um Salamah was one of the wives of the Prophet who brought him several step-children. Though the family of her first husband could have taken the children, they were not Muslim and she considered this situation in the best interest of her children.

When no family member is available to become a guardian for an orphan, other members of the community are considered. Childless couples should consider the blessings they could receive from adoption before resorting to divorce or very expensive medical procedures to have a child of their own.

There are several Qur'anic verses concerning the property of orphans. If an orphan has an inheritance, the child needs someone to look after that wealth until the child reaches adulthood. Among these are:

Don't entrust those who are immature with the property that Allah provided for you as a support. Instead, feed and clothe them (from your resources) and speak to them kindly. Evaluate (the level of maturity) of orphans when they reach a marriageable age. When you determine that they're able to handle the responsibilities (of managing their affairs alone), then release their property to them. Don't be wasteful with their wealth nor spend it rapidly before they reach maturity. If the guardian is rich, then let him claim no compensation. If he's poor, then he can claim a reasonable portion….
Those who unjustly consume the property of orphans only fill their bellies with fire, and for (their callousness they'll soon be made) to roast in a raging blaze! (Qur'an 4:5-10)

When they ask you about orphans, tell them, "The best thing you can do is to help them. If you're their guardian, and you happen to mix your affairs with theirs, (never forget) that they're your brothers, (so keep track of their goods faithfully). (Qur'an 2:220)

The prophet had a special tenderness for orphans:

*"I and the one who looks after an orphan will be like this in Paradise,"
and he gestured with his middle and index fingers with a slight gap
between the two. (Bukhari, Muslim)*

*"Whoever raises three orphans is like the one who spends his nights in
prayer and fasts during the day, and goes out morning and evening
drawing his sword in the cause of Allah. In Paradise, he and I will be
brothers like these two sisters, and he held up his forefinger and middle
finger together." (Ibn Majah)*

*"The best house among the Muslims is one which contains an orphan who
is well treated, and the worst house among the Muslims is one which
contains an orphan who is badly treated" (Ibn Majah).*

With all the respect Islam shows for the bonds of family relationships, it is
not surprising that any act which casts doubt on the paternity of the child
is forbidden. Accordingly, closed adoption, as has often been practiced in
the West, is prohibited. Closed adoption hides the names of the parents
and circumstances of the child's birth and the child is inserted into an
adoptive family, given the name of the family and full inheritance rights,
and the fact of the adoption is often hidden.

While Islam protects the natural family, it also protects the adopting
family from delusions. Adoptive parents can get so attached to a child
whom they love that they create a fiction around him and deny the reality
of his not being their own biological child. They may create a fantasy of
relationship: "He has my eyes, his father's nose" and so on. When the fact
of adoption is concealed, if the parents do not do this themselves, other
people around them may, and the children also do it as they grow up. This
is normal, but it can cause great pain in an adoptive family once the lie is
unmasked. Many stories attest to the long, difficult searches made by
people to find their biological parents.

It may be best if adoptive parents (or step parents) ask the child to call
them "Aunt" and "Uncle" rather than "Mom" and "Dad" although some
scholars say using the names "Mom' and "Dad" as acts of affection, and

calling the child "son" or "daughter" is allowed as long as there are other ways that the lineage of the child is not hidden. Since the first people to be considered as adopting parents are the close relatives of the child, the people may, in fact, be an aunt and uncle or grandparents.

Closed adoption can result in worse harm. Though unlikely today, one strong traditional fear has been that a man might marry his sister or half-sister out of ignorance. Another concern is that medical histories can be inaccurate and cause delays in testing and diagnosis. "No one in my family has ever had breast cancer, Doctor." Not in the adoptive family. But in the biological family there may be a genetic tendency and a grandmother and an aunt who died of it. DNA testing is allowing people to find out all kinds of surprises about their families.

Islam encourages open adoption, with the clear understanding by all involved that the adopted child is the biological child of someone other than the parents of the family. She is called by her father's name and inherits from her birth family automatically, but not from the adopting parents unless they specifically leave her something in their wills. (And up to one third of a person's wealth can be designated for this in a will.) Adoptive parents can also give any amount of wealth, like setting up a trust fund, for the adopted child during their lives.

Some scholars have allowed adoption with change of last name to the name of the adoptive parents in countries where that is the only legal form of adoption and when the greater good of providing a good home for the child outweighs the bad of changing the child's last name. It is still necessary to allow the child and family to know the child's real name if it is knowable and the adoption should not be hidden.

Call (your adopted children) by the surnames of their fathers, for that's the right thing to do in the sight of Allah. However, if you don't know (the surnames) of their fathers, then call them your brothers in faith and your protected ones. (Qur'an 33:5)

A common concern about foster care and adoption voiced in the Muslim community centers around children growing up together who are not mahram (so technically under Islamic law they could marry when they grow up), and the awkwardness of providing privacy in the home.

Traditionally, women have given their breast milk to a child to drink, to make the child mahram for the family. Mahram means related in a way that makes marriage forbidden. (See Qur'an 4:23, 24:31) Nursing a baby five times is considered necessary to establish this relationship. In the modern world today this is rarely an option, but other options exist.

Women don't need to cover themselves before children. So for young children, a family or childless couple can open their doors. As children age, thoughtful arrangements can be made as necessary. Older children are generally so absorbed in school and activities during the day, that the times when they come home and are in close contact with family are short and not hard to manage. The house might even be big enough that separate apartments can be arranged to create more privacy. If parents see there is a problem developing, other living arrangements may need to be set up, like boarding school or housing with grandma. Families can also choose to adopt children of the same sex as their children or of very different ages from their children. When we strive to do good for Allah, He will make it easy on us and show us the best way, Insha Allah.

Another common concern, though less often voiced, is that orphans and foster children for whom family cannot be found must be children of bad people, and likely to grow up bad themselves. We should assume the best when we don't know, not the worst. Why don't we imagine good about the parents rather than bad? So many children are suffering today from wars and political upheaval around them and they need homes. But even if the child came into this world because of a rape or is alone in the world because parents are in prison, this concern has no basis in Islam. The sins of the parent are not inherited by the child. As the Qur'an says above, if you don't know the father of a child, "call them your brothers [or sisters] in faith and your protected ones". Each child is born pure in the nature that Allah gave to him or her. It is part of the tests for our society that we rise to the need to provide for each child in our community.

The Death of a Child

There are many hadith that can give comfort to a parent who has lost a child. These are a few of them:

'When a child of the servant (of Allah) dies, Allah says to the angels, "Have you taken My servant's child?" They reply, "Yes." He says, "Have you taken the fruits of his work." They reply, "Yes." So He says, "What did My servant say?" They reply, "He praised you and mentioned that to You is the return." So Allah says, "Build a house in Paradise for My slave, and name it 'the house of praise.'" (Tirmidhi)

"No woman among you will lose her three children without there being a screen for her from the Fire." Then a woman among them said, "Oh Messenger of Allah, what if two?" She repeated her question twice, and then he said, "And even two, even two, even two!" (Bukhari, Muwatta)

A hadith in Muslim adds that a child who dies will cling to his or her parents until Allah allows them all to enter Paradise.

Someone asked the Prophet (s), "Who are in Paradise?" He replied, "Prophets are in Paradise, martyrs are in Paradise, infants are in Paradise, and children buried alive are in Paradise." (Abu Dawud)

It is a great hardship in this life to lose a child. Allah knows our suffering and will reward us for that loss of joy and dreams. As the Prophet (s) said,

The believing man or woman continues to have affliction in person, property and children so that they may finally meet Allah, free from sin. (Mishkat, by Tirmidhi)

3 - MODELING

Now that we have the basic framework for parents and their children following the world view described in Qur'an and hadith, we will explore teaching methods that have been pulled from the same sources, examples from Prophet Muhammad (s) and how he taught people as well as advice from the Qur'an. These may be summarized briefly as follows:

- Modeling a positive example,
- Rewarding positive behavior through praise, attention, and treats.
- Teaching desired behavior by talking and working together in a constructive manner.
- Decreasing inappropriate behavior by ignoring it, modifying the environment, substituting other action, and allowing natural consequences to occur.

We will start by considering modeling. It is central to raising a Muslim child. The other methods compliment it, encouraging good behavior and discouraging other behavior.

Allah (swt) has built modeling into the basic nature of the child, who copies those around him. Salem, age 3, walks with the same stride as his father, hands behind his back. Mariam pats her little brother on the head and helps him up after a fall. "That's OK", she coos softly, just like Mommy. Some of the behaviors children pick up and copy won't be seen until they are adults with their own spouses. Often a man will treat his wife like his father treated his mother. No one taught him that directly. He just absorbed it. Parents, or surrogate parents are the strongest role models for children. It's a default setting Allah created in children.

We give children additional role models when we teach them about the Prophets and the companions. Remember the image of Mary crying to Allah for help with her delivery as she experiences the contractions of labor and how Allah provides for her? He sends her water, from a small stream and He provided dates ready to pick in the tree over her head. But she needs to make effort herself to shake the tree and to get the water. What an inspiring model of courage in difficulty and how we must make effort to receive help. Think of Joseph cast off by his brothers to become a slave, then after all his good efforts and work, imprisoned for a crime he didn't commit. He was strong in adversity and, in the end, Allah rewarded him with a high position in Egypt and brought his father and family back to him. What an example of patience and persistence for a child!

In the Muslim home, morals, manners, and religious practices may best be taught by modeling. However, it should be obvious that modeling won't work if we, the parents, do not provide sound models. We are expected to practice our religion before trying to tell our children to practice it.

Some parents take their children to the school at the mosque to learn to read Qur'an and pray. But the children never see their parents reading Qur'an and the parents only pray on rare occasions, like when Grandpa comes to visit and organizes the prayers. The example of the parents' actions is far more powerful than all of the words they preach. In such situations parents may be modeling hypocrisy to their children. "Do as I say and not as I do."

Will you ask other people to be righteous, but then forget your own selves? You study the scriptures, so why won't you understand? (Qur'an 2:44)

A man will be brought on the Day of Resurrection and thrown into the Fire, and his intestines will come out in the Fire and he will go around as a donkey goes around its millstone. Then the inhabitants of the Fire will gather around him and say, "Oh such-and-such, what is wrong with you? Did you not enjoin on us what was good and forbid what was bad?" He will say, "I used to enjoin on you what was good but did not do it myself, and I forbade you what was bad but did it myself." (Bukhari)

Muslims have been using modeling since the companions gathered with their children around the Prophet so that their children could learn Qur'an, follow the prayer and fast, and learn to be Muslims with their parents. Muslims don't separate their world into a children's realm and a parent's realm. They lived as families, working and growing together. Our modeling is having children learn while doing with their family.

Modeling is a method that doesn't occur in a vacuum. While showing the child how to do something, and letting the child model it, we also talk to her about it and explain it to her. We can encourage the behavior with rewards and discourage her going off in another direction with a change in the environment or allowing her to experience a natural consequence. We will be using all of the teaching techniques mixed together. What follows are examples of lessons that can be taught by modeling as a primary focus, but with support from other strategies, rewarding positive behavior, direct instruction, and modifying inappropriate behaviors.

Many morals are absorbed by the child through modeling.

Gratitude

For example: It is good manners to say thank you when someone does something good for you. We learn gratitude when we live in an environment where people express their thanks.

If someone is given something, he should give a return for it provided he can afford; if he cannot afford, he should praise him. He who praises him for it, thanks him, and he who conceals it is ungrateful to him. (Abu Dawud, Tirmidhi)

Ashraf models the behavior, thanking people in front of his child, 3-year-old Maysoon, for the nice visit they had together. Later he thanks Maysoon, "You brought me a glass of water. Thank you." Another time he tells her, "You helped me sweep the floor. Thank you." Then when someone gives a present to Maysoon he coaches her, "Tell Auntie thank you, Maysoon", and continues to encourage her until she models the behavior. Ashraf can add to the lessons by including du'a with Maysoon and encouraging her to think of something she is grateful for, to thank Allah while adding something he is grateful for as well.

Be thankful to Allah. Whoever is thankful, then it's to the good of his own soul, but whoever is ungrateful, (know that) Allah doesn't need anything and is (already being) praised. (Qur'an 31:12)

Over time, Maysoon will absorb the manners of gratitude. She will also pick up on her father's feelings and the feelings of others and build her own understanding of why people follow these manners. As she matures, she will be able to understand the deeper meaning of gratitude. So there are two forms of modeling, performing in front of the child and helping the child to do the behavior herself as a learning experience.

Remorse

Allah the Almighty said, "Oh child of Adam, so long as you call upon Me and ask of Me, I shall forgive you for what you have done, and I shall not mind. Oh child of Adam, were your sins to reach the clouds of the sky and were you then to ask forgiveness of Me, I would forgive you. Oh child of Adam, were you to come to Me with sins nearly as great as the earth and were you then to face Me, ascribing no partner to Me, I would bring you forgiveness nearly as great as it." (Hadith Qudsi from Tirmidhi)

Learning to identify wrongdoing and express and learn remorse can be started when children are in the older toddler age. Little Sarah picked up Maysoon's bunny which was lying on the floor. Maysoon ran over and grabbed it from her and hit her with it, knocking her down. Sarah starts crying. Maysoon hugs her bunny and yells, "Mine!" Ashraf orders Maysoon to apologize. Both children are too small to understand apology but it is a start at modeling. Ashraf may decide to give Sarah another similar toy or may require Maysoon to hand over the bunny with the apology. It depends on how special this bunny is to Maysoon.

Requiring Maysoon to say, "Sorry" shows her that there is a code of conduct outside of her that she has not followed, and she did something other people think is wrong. She may say "sorry" with very bad grace and no feeling for the meaning of the word, but this is modeling, learning by doing. Ashraf should also model the behavior himself, apologizing to Sarah and asking her if she got hurt by the bunny. He can model it in other ways at other times, apologizing to Maysoon and her mother if he is late coming home. If he accidently knocked down a tower Maysoon built with blocks, he can apologize and offer to help her rebuild it.

Over time, with multiple occasions to apologize, and with chances to hear her parents also apologize to her and to others, and with simple discussion from time to time, Maysoon will learn the we have to ask for forgiveness when we do something the world feels is wrong. She will pick up on the feelings people seem to have when they apologize. She will also learn to recognize when she has done something wrong or hurt someone. Hopefully she will gradually develop feelings of remorse and empathy with her victim.

It's a slow process but when the environment is set up by the parents, it all unfolds naturally. As she grows, she learns about hurt done to those who aren't with her. She hurt her older brother by eating his dessert before he got home from work, even though she didn't see or hear him complain. She should learn to apologize to him when she sees him later. Mom may need to remind her.

Older children learn to ask forgiveness from Allah (swt). Allah has rules for us to follow and we need to seek forgiveness of Him when we break those rules.

In addition to asking forgiveness, Allah wants us to make amends for our bad conduct. Referring to the first example above, Sarah is a guest in the house and needs something to play with while she is there. After Maysoon says, "Sorry", Ashraf can tell Maysoon that Sarah wants a toy to play with and ask her to show Sarah some toys. He will need to be clear with her (and Sarah) that it is for playing with, not for taking home. He could tell her to let Sarah play with the bunny. But if it is the special bunny that Maysoon always uses to calm herself and to sleep with, it might well be less difficult for her to find another toy for Sarah rather than be forced to share her beloved bunny. In addition to teaching the child to do something good after doing something bad, there is also a lesson in sharing and treating guests with good manners involved here.

Some parents help their children prepare their toys before guests come over. They see that a few significant toys are placed out of reach or out of view and age appropriate toys are out, talking with their children about what their guests might like to do and how to share their toys. This way Jordan's Lego spaceship he spent hours building isn't down where some young guests might break it apart in two minutes. And this way, children are prepared mentally ahead of time to the idea that we share with guests.

Sadaqah (charity)

Sadaqa is due on every joint of a person, every day the sun rises.
Administering of justice between two men is also a sadaqah. And assisting
a man to ride upon his beast, or helping him load his luggage upon it, is a
sadaqah; and a good word is a sadaqah; and every step that you take
towards prayer is a sadaqah, and removing of harmful things from the
pathway is a sadaqah. (Muslim)

"Your smiling in the face of your brother is charity. Commanding good
and forbidding evil is charity. Your giving directions to a man lost in the
land is charity for you. Your seeing for a man with bad eye-sight is a
charity for you. Your removal of a rock, a thorn or a bone from the road
is charity for you. Your pouring what remains from your bucket into the
bucket of your brother is charity for you." (Tirmidhi)

Being thoughtful of others, helping others, these are very basic concepts in
our religion, and we start teaching them to our children as soon as they can
help. First we start with people they know or can see.

In addition to sharing toys with guests, food is an easy thing to share.
Children can help serve guests. They can help prepare plates of cookies to
take over to the neighbors. They can watch Mom and their aunt share a
slice of cake and Grandma share a recipe with a friend.

The Prophet said, "Every Muslim has to give in charity." The people
asked, "Oh Allah's Prophet! If someone has nothing to give, what will he
do?" He said, "He should work with his hands and benefit himself and
also give in charity (from what he earns)." The people further asked, "If he
cannot find even that?" He replied, "He should help the needy who appeal
for help." Then the people asked, "If he cannot do that?" He replied,
"Then he should perform good deeds and keep away from evil deeds and
this will be regarded as charitable deeds." (Bukhari)

There are many things in life we learn by doing. Giving to others is often
one of those things. Sharing with others, being generous, having empathy
for others, these develop on their own, but they develop better and more
richly when children are asked to engage in giving behaviors. The first
reason many children give is because they are asked and they want to

please the person who asked. Being able to identify with the need of someone else, to put yourself in the shoes of someone else, is a complex concept. It develops slowly. Even adults have trouble with it. So, we give sadaqah because Allah said to and He will reward us for it.

Abdu is at school and the boy next to him doesn't have a pencil. Abdu has several and passes him one. The boy thanks him and smiles. Abdu feels warm inside as Allah rewards him with good feelings. And he has made a friend, for future good times.

As children grow, they may gather many toys. They can select some good toys to donate to the poor. These should be nice toys, maybe some present received that the child rarely plays with and is still in good shape. If a child receives lots of presents at one time for an occasion, perhaps he or she might donate something new from among the presents.

But sadaqah is not just things or money. There are hundreds of things children can learn to do as sadaqah. Grandma needs help in the garden; go do some weeding with her. Daddy is working in his home office. Could you take him some coffee? Your sister fell and skinned her knee. She's okay now, but could you find a game to play with her? Allah will reward you for being kind and helping others.

Teaching children sadaqah prepares them to give zakah when they are older and have the means to pay.

Adab (manners)

Prophet Muhammad is described in Qur'an as someone with "**excellent character**". (Qur'an 68:4) And he is also described as "**a beautiful example (to follow) for anyone who longs for Allah and the Last Day and who remembers Allah often**. (Qur'an 33:21) There are multiple examples of his good manners and moral character in hadith and some in Qur'an. We are encouraged to adopt these virtues.

Allah's Messenger (s) neither talked in an insulting manner nor did he ever speak evil intentionally. He used to say, "The most beloved to me amongst you is the one who has the best character and manners." (Bukhari)

There are many manners described in Qur'an and hadith. It is not the focus of this book to describe each one and how to teach it to our children. Manners are best taught by modeling them for our children and coaching them in their efforts to practice and learn them. Only a few examples will be presented here with a few comments.

When someone gives you a greeting, reciprocate with a nicer greeting than that or one equally as nice, for Allah is keeping track of all things. (Qur'an 4:86)

The (true) servants of the Compassionate are those who walk humbly through the earth. Whenever the ignorant try to engage them (in futile argument), they say to them "Peace". (Qur'an 25:63)

These are two examples from Qur'an. Examples from hadith:

"The rights of a Muslim on the Muslims are five: to respond to the salaam, to visit the sick, to follow the funeral processions, to accept an invitation, and to reply to those who sneeze. (Bukhari).

"The young should greet the old, the passerby should greet the sitting one, and the small group of persons should greet the large group of persons." (Bukhari)

The big category of adab, or manners, takes time to learn and some manners might need updating, but they are more than just ethnic customs from long ago. Allah has described manners in Qur'an because they are of benefit to all people. The command above that we respond to greetings is part of a whole system in Islam of how we treat people with a basic level of respect whether we know them or not, whether we like them or not. Allah is giving us a system of manners that set up an environment where people can talk to each other, get to know each other.

In the second quote from Qur'an we see how Allah requires us to be polite to those who want to waste time in empty talk and arguments that have no value. If we don't value what a person is talking about, we should still be polite. Following this advice prevents us from acting in an arrogant way, telling someone off or showing off our own intelligence or knowledge.

Modesty and humility are important moral values. This advice on manners supports those values. The hadith listed here supplement this system of manners that support moral goals. We owe certain basic civil behaviors toward other people. Manners and moral character are both required of a Muslim.

In many cultures, manners are used selectively, based on the judgements people make about each other. Is this person socially below or above me? But we are not supposed to judge others like that in Islam, for Allah alone has that right. And one of the most important functions of good manners is to protect ourselves and others from acting on our private perceptions and internal judgments of others. Everyone forms opinions about those around him. This is a part of our nature. But Allah wants our behavior to be good, no matter who we are with. The Qur'an doesn't say you respond to a greeting only when you feel like it. It doesn't say you can skip it if you don't like the person. It is an obligation of the adab of Islam, the manners of a Muslim. But we do have the right to protect ourselves as well and seek justice when someone has harmed us.

Here is an example of the Prophet when he hosted someone he didn't like:

A man asked permission to enter upon the Prophet. When the Prophet (s) saw him, he said, "What an evil brother of his tribe! And what an evil son of his tribe!" When that man sat down, the Prophet (s) behaved with him in a nice and polite manner and was completely at ease with him. When that person had left, Aisha said (to the Prophet). "Oh Allah's Messenger! When you saw that man, you said so-and-so about him, then you showed him a kind and polite behavior, and you enjoyed his company?" Allah's Messenger (s) said, "Oh Aisha! Have you ever seen me speaking bad or dirty language? (Remember that) the worst people in Allah's sight on the Day of Resurrection will be those whom the people leave (undisturbed) to be away from their evil (deeds)." (Bukhari, Tirmidhi)

The Prophet treated the man well. Maybe because of the good reception he got from the Prophet, the man might think about his message and maybe convert, or at least improve his behavior toward the Prophet or other Muslims. The door is open for the man to improve. Even if he doesn't, Allah, the angels, and the people who observe the Prophet know that he is a person of good manners and morals. Allah rewards us for this

71

and brings us closer to Him. If the man was treated badly by the Prophet, he would have left angry and ready to retaliate. And Prophet Muhammad would have looked like a bad man, not a man close to Allah.

But notice the Prophet didn't allow his good manners to be misinterpreted. He warned Aisha about the man, so she would not assume the Prophet's good manners were a sign that the man was a friend of the Prophet. She knew then not to trust that man and to be careful if she had to deal with him herself. If a person's actions are bad, we may need to protect ourselves from him or her, but Islamic manners prevent us from being unjust and exceeding the limits prescribed by Allah.

All acts are judged according to the intentions behind the acts. When we use good manners, our intentions should be to treat people with the respect due to all human beings. We should not be using the manners to manipulate people. And we need to be observant of our children that they don't fall into that mindset. Do our children use good manners at the mosque and then act rude and mean with people in other settings? Do they use good manners to ask for favors, but speak dismissively when they don't want something? Have they seen us do something like that?

Converts can have a problem transitioning from a life with different manners. They may assume Islamic manners when they are at the mosque or around other Muslims, but when they get out on their own, the social cues around them will trigger their older habits for a while, until they sort things out and make their new manners into habits for all the time.

Children going to non-Islamic environments like schools or other activities may get into a similar situation. They gradually pick up the manners of others so they can fit into the social group. These can conflict with Islamic values. This can have good and bad aspects. The bad aspect is developing habits of speech that are negative, that need to be unlearned. The good aspect is that children get a chance to compare how it feels to use bad manners to the use of good manners when they are home or at the mosque. The good manners of Islam resonate with our fitra and make us feel more at ease.

Standing for Justice

While we want to teach our children to have very good morals and manners, we must not forget that the world is full of difficult people and situations. There will be bullies to deal with. There will be liars. And there will be people who try to oppress others. Our children need to learn to deal with these situations too.

While we should act like the Prophet, with good morals and manners, his life is also a study in how to combat oppression. When he was weak and powerless, he had to put up with things like the boycott of his tribe for three years, during which both his wife Khadijah, and his protecting uncle, Abu Talib, died. Through it all he didn't compromise his morals or his manners, or his devotion to Allah.

The Prophet knew when to use which strategy. He sent his followers away from oppression when they couldn't be protected at home, sending some to Abyssinia and later the Prophet led the migration to Medina. But he didn't wait until he had overwhelming forces to stand up and fight. At the battles of Badr and Uhud, the Muslim forces were outnumbered. He positioned his fighters carefully before the battles. When the enemy lay siege to Medina in the Battle of Khandaq, he used the best latest technology for warfare, digging the trenches. He also taught his people rules of conduct in war, that uphold moral character and good manners, that protect the soul of the soldiers, that have been a model for people ever since. Every soldier was once a small child who was taught how to stand up for himself or herself.

Some people think encouraging their children to fight among themselves and with other children will toughen them up and prepare them to defend themselves in the world. But while it is important that children learn to settle their differences without parents stepping in to play referee, they need us to teach them the rules of behavior first. For that we need to model to them and modeling starts when they are small.

All you who believe! Stand up firmly for justice as witnesses before Allah and (be fair witnesses even if it's) against your own selves, your parents or your relatives, as well. (Also be fair), whether it's (against) the rich or the poor, for Allah can best protect (the legitimate

interests) of both sides. **Don't follow your own whims, for only then can you (judge) with fairness. If you distort (the truth) or fail to do justice, then know that Allah is well-informed of whatever you do. (Qur'an 4:135)**

Children watch as we show them what is fair. Hasna and Jamil both get new backpacks for school but Lianna will use her old one because it is in good enough condition. All children get equal dessert after supper. They go to bed at the same time at night. But their older brother gets to stay up later, because he is in high school. Like this, children learn that there is a system to life which adults follow. Children develop a world view about how the world should work and if something happens that is out of step with that, they see how people step up to fix the issue. They get the chance themselves to correct problems or to ask their parents to correct problems.

Their mother listens to them when they have a dispute. She may pass a fair judgment or, if there is time and reason for it, she may ask them how they want it settled and guide them toward working out an agreement themselves.

Listening to them is important. A child needs to feel authorities listen. If a child knows adults listen in the home, he will expect it outside the home and feel more comfortable speaking up for himself when a problem happens.

Some people consider a child speaking up to be disrespectful and they may be upset by it. But people spoke up to the Prophet and challenged him, sometimes in very disrespectful ways. He allowed it and treated them well in spite of it.

Narrated Abdullah, "Once the Prophet (s) distributed something among his followers. A man said, "This distribution has not been done (with justice) seeking Allah's Countenance." I went to the Prophet (s) and told him (of that). He became so angry that I saw the signs of anger on his face. Then he said, "May Allah bestow His Mercy on Moses, for he was harmed more (in a worse manner) than this; yet he endured patiently."" (Bukhari)

It is best if children speak up respectfully, but they don't always know how. While they are learning that, we need to have patience with them, like Muhammad (s) and Moses (s).

With young children, we need to be aware of their development. Most children have no problem separating what happened from what they wished or feared. We can depend on them for a clear explanation of what happened as soon as they have sufficient vocabulary. However, there is a wide variation in children's verbal ability, how many words they know to describe things and how well they organize facts. A child who is bilingual may be a bit slower at these tasks too. A child who is slow to explain things and stumbles around may be trying to remember a word or trying to puzzle out what exactly happened, because he wasn't really focusing on events until someone started yelling.

It's important to give children many opportunities to speak and describe their day or tell stories, as well as expose them to many stories to enrich their vocabularies. These activities help children become more effective in organizing their ideas and speaking up clearly to stand up for themselves in the world.

Before the age of six or so, some children have trouble separating fact from fiction or organizing a chronology of what happened. They can mix the two up in their story of what happened without having any intention of lying.

Four-year-old Hassan told his mother, "Banan told me I could borrow her pencil and then she hit me for taking it." Actually, he hadn't asked her if he could borrow the pencil but she had let him use it a few days ago while she was doing her homework. So even though he's not supposed to get into her schoolbag, he felt it was okay to get out the pencil. He's not able to clarify or be aware of the difference between permission given earlier and permission given today. Then Hassan got scared when Banan yelled at him for taking her pencil. She grabbed it back from him, hurting his hand a little. His fear magnified the event, so he called that a "hit".

Confusing facts like this in telling a story is common in four-year-olds with their limited verbal skills. When children wish things, expect things, or are very fearful of things, they can present them in a story as the truth.

They gradually outgrow this. If they are able to tell stories and listen to others tell stories, this can help them learn to separate fact from imagination. They also learn what is important to include in a story to make it meaningful and what they can leave out. Adults can get very tired of listening to a child meander through a story that seems to have no point. We need to coach the child to come to some point—and ask for specific details to clarify the story and improve their storytelling ability.

It can be complicated for a parent to sort all this out. "Did Banan tell you that right now?" "Show me how she hit you?" Banan is seven and will be much more able to explain her side of the story and show how she took the pencil. Calmly and nicely, Mom can clarify Hassan's story with him until it reflects what actually happened. Then they can talk about why permission yesterday is different from permission today. Banan needs to apologize for grabbing too. She should have asked nicely to have her pencil back.

Children will tell lies too, of course. It is part of learning how the system works. It is important in standing up for our rights that we be truthful and don't exaggerate. Modeling this behavior and guiding our children through the murky waters of distinguishing between covering faults and telling the truth is a slow process but very important.

To stand up for justice for themselves or for others, children need to know what justice is too. They need to know how the system of expressing a complaint works, as well as being able to present their case. Children need opportunities to play games with rules that they can enforce themselves. They need to see Mom challenge an error at the store cash register and Dad discuss a difference of opinion with his brother.

Children will also learn important lessons if we stand up for causes in our community that we feel are important. The water in our community has been polluted by a factory near town. We can join in the protest. Children can attend demonstrations and help make signs. They can help distribute bottled water to affected homes. Standing up for justice for ourselves is one thing. It is also important to stand up for justice for others as well, no matter who they are.

This complex issue takes a lot of time to learn and children will make errors as they learn. Gently and gradually we encourage them so they can stand up to the difficulties life will bring them, with good manners and without resorting to immoral acts, and fight for what is right for themselves and others in the community.

Respect for Religion

We teach respect for religion first by modeling respectful behavior to our children and then by watching over them as they model the behavior until they can do it correctly. But what exactly are we teaching them?

Respect for religion is a general attitude but also a way of speaking and acting. Every culture has always developed customs to deal with subjects it values. Nationalist countries have elaborate rules about how to handle the national flag and how to respect different figures in the government. Religions of the world all have things they do to show their respect to their deity, houses of worship, religious leaders, and holy books and other objects of veneration. In the current secular environment many Muslims live in today, the customs for respecting religions have been falling into disuse.

Not long ago, it was common in America to capitalize pronouns in print when they referred to God. Now that habit is being more and more ignored. The celebrations of the birth and death of Prophet Jesus (s), so important to the dominant Christian population, have been turned into great commercial shopping and partying events with less and less focus on the religious aspect of the holidays. Muslims often find their children pick up the general disrespect of religions from the culture outside their home.

Children might refer to the prophets generally as "those guys" without recognizing or intending any disrespect. A child might be heard reciting the Qur'an in the bathroom, memorizing a surah (chapter of Qur'an) as he took a shower. Many parents, particularly new converts, are so used to the general society that they often don't recognize disrespectful behavior themselves.

In many places of the Muslim world a mushaf, or copy of the Qur'an in Arabic, is placed with honor on the top of a bookshelf, never lower. It is handled with loving care and kissed. It never goes on the floor or has something placed over it. No one touches it unless they have wudu (ritual washing for prayer). A copy of a translation of Qur'an without the Arabic might be treated with less respect but still handled nicely.

Places that are unclean, or where serious washing takes place, like bathrooms, are separated from places that are clean. And the Qur'an, reciting Qur'an, discussing religion, and praying, are given the cleanest areas of the house. That's part of why Muslims often use prayer rugs, to make sure the area where we pray is very clean, even though technically we can pray in the dirt. It's also why shoes for outside are never worn inside the house.

The specific actions people do may not be directly from Qur'an or hadith, but they are often linked in some way, particularly to hadith. Many are derived from general ideas. There were no copies of the Qur'an in the time of the Prophet and likely no bookshelves either. But out of the love people had for Allah and their faith, they built up cultural norms of behavior to act on their sense of respect.

Most cultural traditions can simply be learned and continued wherever someone is in the Muslim world. They add to the sense of community of Muslims. However, in regions of the world where there is no established tradition, like in America, a fluid social situation exists. A new American convert may find that his Pakistani-American neighbor does one thing, but his Somali-American neighbor does something else. The convert can decide what works best for his family and twenty-first century American life. He should discuss these topics with friends and family. Muslims live in community and we should work with our community to update, develop, and pass on ways to be respectful. In the multi-ethnic melting pot of American Muslims, a blend of customs will probably result.

We should always use the best language when talking about the religion, like we use the best language when talking to people. But this doesn't mean we can't ask questions or voice criticism respectfully. We should. It's part of the learning process. And because of previous eras in history where people were encouraged to follow their scholars blindly, memorizing without questioning, there are some doubtful if not incorrect things that have been passed down as Islamic information by very pious, well-intentioned people.

Showing respect for religion also means being careful to separate fairy stories from religious stories, and keep religious stories free of fanciful embroidery. This can be difficult. Muslims have been lax in this area for centuries and many Islamic children's books from Muslim countries include colorful details in the stories of the prophets, jinn, and angels that are not from Qur'an and hadith. In part this is because there often aren't enough details to flesh out a "good story". With many children, just telling them often that these are stories for fun and not real is enough. But some children do get confused and the confusion can exist for years without parents knowing.

An important part of respecting religion is to oversee that children get correct information. When little Joey asks his mother if Allah made their car, she needs to answer him seriously, not brush him off. People make cars but they use the iron and oil and other raw materials Allah provided them. If Karima worries about shoes being left upside down, because her Islamic Studies teacher told her it's disrespectful to Allah to turn the soles of the shoes toward Allah, Dad needs to consider discussing where Allah actually is and why 'up' is not a reasonable response. He also needs to talk to the teacher. This is an old wives' tale, not good Islamic instruction. We want our shoes to be placed neatly when we remove them so we can find them easily, so no one stumbles over them, and perhaps so things look nice, but not because Allah might be insulted by how we place them.

Speak politely with your children, no matter their age, and take their concerns seriously. They will be encouraged to discuss more often. They will notice how their parent follows up with a teacher who has taught something strange or an imam who says something odd from the mimbar (the podium in a mosque).

Being respectful doesn't mean we have to be super serious about everything. A two-year-old tried to do a call to prayer and sang out "Alahbaba" instead of "Allahu Akhbar." Smile with a chuckle and thank him. Repeat "Allahu Akhbar" with him a few times and tell him "Good job". And we need to appreciate the imagination of storytellers.

Cinderella and Batman are fun. We just need to be clear with children about what is real and what is imaginary.

A parent needs to model respectful behavior herself and correct her children to do the same. If this is started when they are small, whenever it comes up, it is much more easily done. If someone is starting when the children are older, and all the family has old bad habits, we need to have lower expectations. Gradually trying to practice new habits and discussing this change with our children will get the family moving in a healthier direction Insha Allah. With teen children, we may have to accept that they have to decide to change on their own.

Taharah (cleanliness)

One of the first concepts of Islam that a child will learn is probably taharah, because we wash our children from the time they are born. The way we keep them clean and teach them to keep themselves clean is directly related to our faith.

The Prophet (s) said, "Cleanliness is half of faith . . . " (Muslim)

The key to Paradise is prayer and the key to prayer is cleanliness (wudu). (Mishkat, by Ahmad)

There are very specific instructions in hadith about how to use the toilet and how to make things clean. Urine and feces are dirty and we must clean them from our bodies by washing with water. We want our children to be as clean as we are. To clean up small children's accidents we have the hadith:

The urine of a female (child) should be washed and the urine of a male (child) should be sprinkled over until the age of eating. (Abu Dawud)

The difference between female babies and male babies that is made here is probably because the boy tends to spray out urine while the girl make puddles that are easier to clean. That doesn't happen today with diapers but it was an issue with the way babies were handled centuries back. Today we just clean any baby with water or other liquid cleaner at every diaper change. As the child gets older we can wash the child over the toilet and teach the child to do this himself or herself as they grow in ability. This is in addition to the general habits of all people to wash hands after using the toilet.

Boys should be trained to urinate sitting. Standing increases the chance of urine getting sprayed where it isn't supposed to be. There is a specific hadith about this.

The Messenger of Allah (s) saw me urinating while standing. At that, he said, "Umar, do not urinate while standing." (Ibn Majah)

Children watch their parents do wudu (wash for prayer) and their parents coach their efforts as they slowly learn. For the details of taharah, direct instruction is needed. We can't model all the details. Children can pick up some of the rules, like when wudu is necessary, just from listening and watching their parents over the years. But a class in an Islamic school or reading a book on the topic will ensure that everything gets covered. It's good for children to learn about periods and wet dreams a little before they reach the age for them. It might be difficult for parents to cover these topics with their children. Taharah is an important topic in a sex education class for Muslims. This education is covered in Chapter 4, Communication Without Taboos.

Dhikr (Remembrance of Allah)

Teaching a child to do dhikr and du'a by giving him or her a lecture is like teaching swimming without going into the pool. We model this behavior and encourage our children to participate with us.

Then remember Me; I shall remember you. (Qur'an 2:152)

Remember Allah often so that you may be successful. (Qur'an 62:10)

Allah Most High says, "I am to My servant as He thinks Me to be, and I am with him when He remembers Me. Then, if he remembers Me within himself, I remember him within Myself; and if he remembers Me in a group of people, I remember him in a group better than them; and if he comes near to Me one span, I go near to him one cubit; and if he comes near to Me one cubit, I go two outstretched arms' distance nearer to him;

81

and if he comes walking to Me, I go running to him." (Bukhari, Muslim)
[Cubit and span are old units of measure; the cubit is longer than the span.]

Many people might associate dhikr with sufi traditions of group or individual hours-long activities spent in reciting du'a. Most children won't have the concentration for this kind of activity, and many adults don't either. That is a very small part of dhikr.

Dhikr and du'a are closely linked. Dhikr is about remembering who Allah is and du'a is more asking or thanking Allah. In a way, du'a includes dhikr because we wouldn't be doing it if we weren't remembering Allah. Though there are ritual times for these acts, like at the end of salah, and special formulas we can learn to say for them, they can also be done in any informal words and any language.

Any time we are taking or thinking about Allah, His abilities, His mercy, His power, we are remembering Him. Talking about Allah with a child helps the child visualize Allah in the environment of the home or the garden, or wherever the family happen to be. "Alhamdulillah (thanks be to Allah), we remembered to bring the umbrella. Look, it's started to rain!" "Masha'Allah (Allah made it) isn't it cool how this spider is making its web. Come see." "Allah made this disease and He made the cure. May He bring you back to health quickly." These kinds of short statements, when we are out at the park, in the garden, or sitting at our sick child's bedside, remind us of Allah in our world and our dependence on Him. We create an environment where Allah feels present for our children and for ourselves.

For a more formal activity of dhikr and du'a, a parent can lead the family in du'a and get everyone to participate, perhaps after salah or as part of a bedtime ritual. Even little children can lift up their hands to Allah, imitating those around them, when a parent recites a du'a. Keep the words simple when children are participating, so that they can understand, and the activity should be short so children don't get bored or distracted and start misbehaving. As different people in the room add their du'as, thanking Allah for things that happened that day and asking for help and guidance for upcoming things, the whole family can feel united in worship and togetherness with Allah.

There are several concerns we need to be careful of when we try to create an environment of remembrance. First and foremost, we need to keep things sincere and not fall into habits of speech that lose meaning.

Some people say, "Insha Allah" as a rote response to any request without registering that they need to change their schedule or behavior to make something happen. "Can you drive me over to my friend's house?" asks Sami. His mother just got home from work and has a list in her head of all she wants to get done this evening, starting with thawing out some food for supper. She responds automatically to her son, "Insha Allah." But she continues to dig out the food from the freezer and put it in the microwave to defrost. Then she goes to do wudu while yelling at her daughter to ask if she's finished any homework. She has no time or energy to get out the car again and drive four miles in rush hour traffic to take her son to his friend's, but she doesn't address that issue. She just brushed off the request and forgot it.

Another concern about dhikr can be in emphasizing one aspect of Allah to the point of forgetting other attributes. Some people focus on the negative. "You eat too much candy. Allah will make all your teeth fall out." "Don't you lie to me! Allah knows when you lie and you'll end up in Hell that way!" The opposite is the parent who over-focuses on Allah's forgiveness and never corrects or punishes the child, no matter how bad the behavior.

The balance between the anger of Allah and His mercy is heavily weighted in favor of mercy, and we should reflect this with our children. Yet there is Hell and the punishment of Allah and we need to keep this in mind as well, to keep us on the straight path. Threatening children with Allah is not one of the management techniques of a good Muslim parent. Letting children do whatever they want is not a technique either. Chapter 6 gives parents strategies for dealing with bad behavior.

Your Lord has written it upon His (Own nature) to be merciful (Qur'an 6:54)

When Allah decreed the Creation He pledged Himself by writing in His book which is laid down with Him: My mercy prevails over my wrath. (Bukhari, Muslim, an-Nasa'i, Ibn Majah)

There are one hundred (parts of) mercy for Allah and He has sent down out of these one part of mercy upon the jinn and human beings and animals and the insects, and it is because of this (one part) that they love one another, show kindness to one another and even the beast treats its young one with affection, and Allah has reserved ninety-nine parts of mercy with which He will treat His servants on the Day of Resurrection. (Muslim)

In creating an environment of remembrance, parents often recite the two surahs of protection, Surah Al Falaq and Surah An Nas (113 and 114) over their children before they go to sleep or if they wake up with a nightmare. It's very calming and can help a child sleep better. A problem can come up if a child has nightmares often and this is the only thing parents offer for help. It can be similar to the situation of a child praying to get an A in tomorrow's test but not studying for the test. Nightmares can be a sign of anxiety in a child, a common problem for adults as well as children, and parents should address the anxiety so children don't decide that Allah doesn't help. Sometimes it's an obvious issue, like living in a war zone or recuperating from a hurricane or earthquake disaster. Then the whole family needs to come together and work through their fears and strengthen each other. Usually it's much more minor, like a scary movie the child saw or bullying at school. We often have to do much more than just pray for help. We have to investigate and do what we can to help ourselves.

In the story of Mary in Qur'an (19:23), she delivered her baby alone and cries out for help. Allah does provide for her but the angel tells her to shake the tree herself to get dates to eat. She has to make efforts herself. And we do, too, in order to receive many of Allah's blessings.

Prayers of all of you are granted provided you do not get impatient and start grumbling that, "I prayed to my Lord but He did not grant me." (Bukhari & Muslim in Riyadh-us-Saleheen)

"There is not a Muslim upon the earth who calls upon Allah with any request, except that Allah grants it to him, or he turns away from him the

like of it in evil; as long as he does not request for something sinful, or the severing of the ties of kinship." (Tirmidhi)

Salah and Du'a (formal and informal prayer)

Muslims get so caught up in teaching salah that they often ignore teaching du'a, informal prayer. But it can be used as a way to grow into learning salah.

It fits well into a going-to-bedtime routine with little children. Latifah raised her hands each night standing beside her daughter Jamilah's crib. She said a simple du'a in her own words asking Allah for a good night's sleep for herself and for her daughter. Then she wiped her hands over herself and turned to her child and stroked the baby's face gently while reciting the two surahs of protection, 113 and 114. Sometimes her daughter slept through the night and sometimes she didn't. As Jamilah got older she started refusing to sleep if Mommy didn't go through this routine. Daddy could act as a replacement sometimes but no one else. As time went on, the parents developed a routine of having one of them do the du'a with Jamilah, asking her to add something of her own, like thanking Allah for the good food she'd had that day or for the sunny day that had led to a visit to the park. With time Jamilah learned her first short surahs and could recite them in her du'a. As she grows, she can learn of all the other times she can make du'a, like before the doctor gives her a shot or when the family gets into the car to take off on vacation. She can participate with other members of the family or by herself. Through modeling she learns how to communicate and develop her relationship with Allah.

Then salah can be taught as a formal way of communicating with Allah. If we were going to meet the president or the king of our country, we would want to dress well, to be clean and look our best. We would want to speak well, in a manner that sounds good. Yes, we can speak to a king or president in our work clothes when he or she happens to pass by. But when we have an appointment to speak, we want to present our best foot forward.

Five times a day, we have an appointment to speak in the presence of our Lord. We wash ourselves and make the prayer place clean and neat. We recite some Qur'an and du'a in Arabic. We bow and prostrate ourselves before the divine, reminding ourselves to be humble before the power that is so much greater than we are. We speak in the most eloquent manner that we can, adding our own du'a. Rather than a quick du'a in the locker room, "Oh Allah help me and my team win today", we may thank Allah for the strength and health He has given us and thank Him for allowing us to play at our best to support our team well. There are several places in the salah where personal du'a can be added but when we are following the imam in group salah, the easiest place is at the end. Teaching the child salah as a more ceremonial form of du'a makes salah much more meaningful and puts all the details into better perspective.

We model salah to our children every time we pray in their presence as well as when they see us preparing for salah and talking about it. "We can't go to the store until I've prayed. So I'll pray just at the beginning of asr (afternoon prayer) and then we will go. We might be late getting back." Witnessing us speaks more clearly than any teacher in a classroom.

Very little children are drawn to this event that happens so often in their house. If a child tries to interfere or gets fussy, a parent can pray while holding him, like Prophet Muhammad (s) held his granddaughter Umamah (r). It is reported in hadith collections Bukhari and Abu Dawud that when he prostrated he would put her down and then he would pick her up when he stood up again.

Toddlers and preschool children often put themselves in line beside a parent or older sibling. It's best to have them stand at the end of a row so they can leave any time they please without bothering anyone. They tend to bow and prostrate to their own rhythm, out of step with others, and they can get turned around a bit but that is fine. Allah will reward them for every small effort. There is no worry about wudu for them or being properly dressed either. Around age 7 we start to expect more participation.

Many parents may have heard an often quoted hadith:

Order your children to observe salat when they reach the age of seven and hit them for not observing it when they reach the age of ten, and arrange their beds (for sleeping) separately. (Abu Dawud)

86

There are some problems with this hadith, however. There is a lot of evidence in other hadiths that puberty, or the age of reason, is the correct age for Allah to hold us accountable for our deeds, including our fasting and salah. So how can the Prophet tell people to hit younger children for not praying? There are hadiths saying the Prophet himself never hit anyone for anything and there are variations of this hadith from other sources which say start the child praying salah at 7 and train him from age 10. This makes more sense to prepare a child to be responsible for the salah by the age of puberty.

Scholars have debated this quandary over the centuries. There have been many scholars who allow the hadith to stand, but caution that any hit not leave a mark on the body or strike tender parts of the body. Other scholars question the authenticity and refuse it, like Dr. Ali Gomaa and Dr. Mohamed Elzoghbe. (The "hit" part of this hadith will be covered in Chapter 6 under the topic: Physical Punishment.)

When a boy distinguishes right hand from the left hand, then command him to pray. (Abu Dawud)

Parents should hope that their children will have the habit of salah by the time Allah starts holding them accountable, puberty. All earlier efforts to pray are part of earning good deeds, establishing good habits.

In a very supportive environment, one parent taught her child salah this way: On his fifth birthday, she asked him to begin regular prayer with the family once a day. This was treated as a special event, a significant landmark on his road to growing up. His mother asked him to pray maghreb (evening prayer), when the whole family was at home and could pray together. Then, when the child reached five and a half, she added a second salah. This could be any out of the five. On the sixth birthday, a third salah was added; at six and a half, the fourth; and by the seventh birthday, he was doing all five prayers regularly.

Some people may have the supportive environment for this schedule. But for many parents in the United States, life isn't very relaxed. Families struggle to get everyone out of the house to work and school each morning. Parents have enough to do to get their own fajr (predawn) prayer done. Family members are gone all day so dhuhr (noon) and often 'asr (afternoon) have to be prayed at work or school. It's hard for parents to find a place and time to pray at work.

At school, unless a child is in an Islamic school, there is no supportive environment. Older children can get permission to pray, but they are doing it completely on their own initiative. Many children are too shy to interrupt the flow of the school day and go off by themselves for this. So maghrib and 'isha (night) are often the only prayers the family can do together at home on the weekdays. When everyone is doing something, it is easier to get children to join. But when children know their friends at school and the neighbor families all don't do salah, when salah can be seen as an interruption to everyday life rather than as a simple activity that everyone does, it becomes much harder. Some suggested methods and details are presented here to inspire parents. Each family will have to figure out what works in their house.

One parent had a few friends and relatives, older adults known to her child, write cards to her. They were asked to say something in the cards about what they got out of salah or why they valued it, along with congratulating the child on growing up and starting salah. These cards gave the child an idea of why people do salah and what she should look for in the prayer. It also gave the child a sense that she was praying with these older adults she cared about, her role models. The child received these cards on her seventh birthday when she was invited to pray one prayer regularly with her family. On the following birthday another prayer was added, and so on each year until all five were being prayed by age twelve.

Another method is to create the expectation that the child will grow up praying by casually mention in the preschool child's presence, as the occasion arises, how some older child prays all his or her prayers regularly. A mention can be made, in the car on the way to the grocery store, or while washing dishes, where parents and others can express their expectations of the child. "Before I was eight I could do all my prayers regularly, without my mommy reminding me," Grandma might be able to say. "It feels so warm and good when we all gather together for salah," Daddy might say. Then the child is called to join any group salah as convenient, while allowed to sit it out sometimes. The motivation to pray will gradually grow in the child, rather than being a chore parents nag about. Gradually the child joins salah with the family. Then with some additional instruction and support, the older child can begin praying salah on his or her own, when parents aren't around. This method is expected to take several years and depends on outside influences being minimal.

Creating the right mood for salah can help all of us. Some parents interrupt their children and expect them to come running immediately, no matter what game is interrupted. This is thoughtless. Ask them when they will be finished with what they are doing and work around that if you can. Make it a discussion with them rather than an order from their parent. We are the parents and we are setting the schedule, but we can ask for input from them and be considerate where possible. Otherwise, with a group of family members to assemble we can have endless fuss over the schedule. Another idea is to have a clock or computer give the call to prayer and establish a family habit of assembling fifteen or twenty minutes after the call is heard every day.

Some children are naturally less organized than others. We may need to just start the salah and hope they join in even if they are late, have forgotten wudu, or a girl has forgotten her scarf. Under the age of puberty, salah is not required but parents have to pray. They don't always have the time to spend waiting for everyone and getting everyone perfectly ready. The children will be rewarded by Allah for their efforts even if they aren't perfect. And we should encourage them. "Abdullahi, you did a good job joining the prayer without bumping into anyone. Did you remember wudu this time? Well remember better for next time."

Keep a prayer calendar up on a wall or someplace where everyone can check the times. Then let older children plan when they are going to pray and let them pray on their own sometimes. Discuss this with them and then remind them of their plans, or help them design their own reminders. This is part of their becoming independent adults. It may be better to pray together, but how are young people going to learn to pray at high school or later at college on their own if they don't learn this independence?

Having a special place in the home for salah is a nice luxury when families have the space. If a room has to serve several purposes, set it up so it is quick and easy to bring out the prayer rugs. Let children help with setup.

Some people like to burn incense to clear the air of cooking odors. Make sure girls have pretty prayer outfits to put on and a convenient place to store them. Arrange the bathroom so it's easy to do wudu.

It is suggested that the child pray only the fard rakats (minimum required units of prescribed prayer movements) at the beginning. Some parents want to add the Sunnah prayers (additional to the required prayers) quickly and since they do them themselves regularly. In a stable, supportive home this may work admirably. However, people differ in their appreciation for different aspects of the religion. Some really enjoy salah and get a strong benefit from it. Others find it hard to concentrate, a chore. At different ages of our lives we may be more drawn to it than at other ages. We don't want to pressure our children so that they turn away from it as soon as they are out of our sight.

If parents are new to Islam or they have a more difficult environment with many other influences on themselves and their children, they need to accept that Allah knows the difficulties they face and will reward them even if they don't feel successful. We need to be good role models for our children. Tell them why it is important to us and what we get out of it. We need to give them simple instructions.

Just learning the prayers in Arabic is difficult for many. Then to add variety to it, we recite different surahs, all in Arabic. Then the timings don't fit well into an American or western cultural time framework. Then we need wudu and a clean quiet place to concentrate. It's a lot. Do small things regularly and build slowly. Relax. Allah knows the intention and the effort and He rewards greatly for that.

It's optional whether we take younger children to the mosque for prayers. If we have someone to care for them at home, it's often better because they can get restless and bored and cause problems that interfere with the prayers of others. Children vary in their ability to sit still through the khutbah (sermon) too. But many mothers want to attend the prayers. Prophet Muhammad was sensitive to this issue and he addressed it:

When I stand up to pray, I want to be long in it, but then I hear the crying of a child and at that I refrain (from this) in my salah, hating to give trouble to its mother (Bukhari, Muslim).

Anas ibn Malik (r) reported, "I never prayed behind any imam a lighter or more complete salat than the Prophet's (s). If he heard the crying of a child, he would make it shorter out of fear of being a trial for its mother." (Bukhari)

People need to use common sense. Test the child and see how he responds. One mother found her baby cried every time the loud microphone at the mosque was used. That child needs to stay home until he is less sensitive to the noise. Another found her children would sit quietly through the khutbah if she took them to a nearby park to play for a while beforehand, so they were ready for a rest by the time she got them to the mosque.

While it is certainly important for men to attend a mosque for salah if they can, a considerate husband will make opportunities for his wife to go to the mosque when she wants to go, while he stays home with the children, as long as his jummah salah (Friday prayer) is not compromised. They can also divide up the children when they go to the mosque, some with him and some with her so the whole family can attend jummah or programs at the mosque. Parents need to work together to balance their needs for their own religious study, their religious devotions, volunteer work in the community, and commitment to their children and family.

There are men who get so focused on the reward for themselves of making their prayers in the mosque and attending study groups there with their friends, that they forget to balance this with the rewards they get for many other responsibilities and obligations, especially seeing to the education of their children. In some countries, the mosque is within short walking distance of neighborhood houses and attending the five prayers there is not difficult. And the schools teach children about religion so parents' responsibilities are very light in this respect. In the United States, this is a dream for most Muslims. For the future of his children's Islam, it is highly recommended that a father teach them religion, make salah with them frequently, and interact closely with them so that they will identify with him and his values.

Siyam (fasting)

Teaching fasting is pretty easy if a family is part of a community that fasts. We fast from all food and water from the beginning of fajr (predawn time), after the meal called suhoor, until the sun sets at maghrib. The iftar, or fast-breaking meal at sunset, becomes a very important time for the family to get together and eat. We often prepare these meals much more carefully than other meals. Each family has traditions about what foods to serve. Some always start with dates and yogurt drink. Some start with a serving of fruit. Some pray maghrib (evening prayer) immediately after a quick drink of water and then sit down to eat. There are special ways people use to determine when the time of maghrib has come.

Children notice these events in their house, in community with others, at a park or at the mosque, or as guests in someone's home. They may notice that we don't eat during the day and that we talk about organizing our days around fasting. "I won't be playing tennis all Ramadan. I need to focus on fasting." "Daddy rescheduled his business trip so it won't interfere with Ramadan." It's normal for many young children, who are used to eating with the family, to refuse to eat their meals when parents don't join them. They may wait until they are really hungry before they finally accept to eat, but they adjust to eating alone.

Since every effort made toward learning something good is rewarded by Allah, people encourage children to learn to fast. It is a sign of maturity when a child can master the self-control to wait for food and water. Parents can test the child. A common way is to challenge the child to fast half days first, from breakfast till lunch and maybe from lunch to iftar. This is basically giving up snacks. When a child can do that easily, try from breakfast to iftar, missing snacks and lunch.

Normal healthy children in Muslim countries, where the rhythm of life adjusts for the month of Ramadan, have no trouble fasting every day, all day long, for the whole month from ages 7 or 8. Since children don't drink coffee or tea, (or smoke), they often fast more easily than adults. In places where summer fasting days are very long and work and school hours inflexible, children may only fast on Mondays and Thursdays or only on weekends, or the first few days of the month and the last few. Children enjoy the challenge of fasting, even if they need a bit of encouragement from time to time during the day. They are proud of their strength. We don't want it to become a burden that they dread. For parents it's a balancing act to find the moderate path in the middle for our children.

A companion's recollection of fasting Ashura, (the day Moses and his people were spared from Pharaoh) with the Prophet included:

"We used to make toys out of wool and took (them to the mosque) along with us. When they (the children) asked us for food, we gave them these toys to play with, and these made them forgetful till they completed their fast." (Muslim)

We, too, can see that our children are kept busy during the day so that they forget they aren't eating. Some physical exercise is good, as long as they don't get dehydrated. A nap in the late afternoon also helps to pass the time.

Many people are lax about waking for suhoor, the predawn meal, but it is very important, particularly for children. It's very hard for a growing child to get enough food and water from only one meal a day. It's not recommended for adults to live on one meal either.

Have suhoor, because truly there is blessing in suhoor. (Bukhari)

It's important to ensure that food served at suhoor is healthy and sustaining. High protein foods are favored, and foods that digest slowly. It's also important to drink enough water. Soups, smoothies, and various health food drinks are useful. We also need to be careful not to overeat. After the first 3 days of fasting, the body adjusts its time clocks and expects food at suhoor but not at noon. We normally feel hunger for the first few days and after that we will be fine with our new eating schedule. Generally, we should not gain or lose weight during Ramadan.

If a child starts getting dehydrated or seems to be getting sick, parents need to tell their child to drink water and resume eating. We need to be thoughtful about this because children may feel like they failed, that they are weak or not good enough. We can remind our child that we don't fast if it would be harmful to ourselves.

93

Allah doesn't want us to get sick from fasting. The most important reason for fasting is to come closer to Him, to clear away the other preoccupations of life and remember our dependence on Him. He also wants us to become strong, to have self-control, so we can handle any other test He might send us in our lives. You need to ask your boss for a raise? You need to start over with your life after a flood has destroyed your house? Allah never gives us something harder than we can bear and we have the strength to get through whatever He sends us.

All you who believe! Fasting is prescribed for you, even as it was prescribed upon those before you, so you can increase your mindfulness (of Allah). .... Fasting is indeed good for you, if you only knew. (Qur'an 2:183-4)

Not everyone can fast. Mothers usually have at least a week off from fasting during their periods. If a parent has an illness that prevents fasting, like diabetes, it can be hard to be a good role model for the child. But teaching the child to fast can be part of this parent's way of experiencing Ramadan, waking and having suhoor with the child, preparing the evening meal together and avoiding eating or drinking in front of the child during the day.

Sometimes it is the child who cannot fast. No one fasts when they are sick—of course. Some children have problems fasting during a growth spurt. If the child seems lethargic or gets dizzy during the day, and a short rest doesn't perk them up, they may need a break from fasting for a day or a few days, until they feel more energetic. It's hard to know when a child is having a growth spurt so we just have to be thoughtful about the possibility.

Some children can't eat large meals or can't adapt to eating suhoor. If the fasting day is very long, as it is in the summer in most of the United States, suhoor might need to be eaten at 3:00 in the morning. It's hard to wake up children at that hour and then get them back to sleep after praying fajr. Children who can't eat a good suhoor or who can't adapt to disrupted sleep should not fast full days like adults. Other children might have blood sugar issues. They aren't diabetic, but in danger of becoming diabetic. And, of course there are children with diabetes who can't fast.

When children can't fast, they can feel left out of the group. We need to help them feel a part of things anyway. One way, like the mother who has her period, is to be the person responsible for helping others to fast. Families can always use helpers. The child who can't fast can be asked to organize a game to keep other siblings occupied while they fast. Everyone can help prepare food. The child who isn't fasting can have the special job of food tester, checking that there is enough salt in the dish. Many families have a Ramadan calendar hung in the dining room or kitchen to mark the days of the month. The child who can't fast might get the responsibility of taking care of the calendar, or of being in charge of announcing to the family when maghrib starts and it is time to break the fast.

Ramadan is not just the month of fasting. It is also the month of Qur'an. Many mosques have Qur'an memorization contests during the month. Parents can start their own contests. Ramadan is also the month for remembering the poor and those who don't have food. Many mosques serve iftar meals every night and do outreach to help the poor. Parents and children can volunteer to help with the iftars or with taking food to the poor. This is also the month of taraweeh prayers, (prayed after 'isha, the night prayer, usually 8 or 20 rakats (units of prescribed prayer movements)) Children can attend taraweeh prayers at the mosque or families can pray these special prayers at home.

Hajj and Umrah (obligatory and voluntary pilgrimage)

Both the parent and the child will receive a reward if the child performs Hajj, the pilgrimage to Mecca.

A woman lifted up her child and said, "Messenger of Allah, will the child be credited with having performed the Hajj?" Thereupon he said, "Yes, and there will be a reward for you." (Muslim, Ibn Majah, An- Nasa'i)

"We performed Hajj with the Messenger of Allah (s), and there were women and children with us. We recited the talbiyah on behalf of the children and stoned the pillars on their behalf." (Ibn Majah)

Scholars agree that the child will need to do Hajj again when he or she becomes adult to fulfill the requirement of doing it at least once in their life, but it is a Hajj experience. Prophet Muhammad (s) encouraged people to take their children with them when they went for Hajj and for hundreds of years whole families travelled together from all over the Muslim world to make this trip.

It can be dangerous to do Hajj today, with the crowding, particularly stoning the pillars. With so many people from all over the world camping together, germs are easily spread too. We need to be very careful to keep healthy and safe, so most people don't recommend taking children on this journey now. However, umrah, the smaller pilgrimage, is much easier to accomplish and is also very rewarding. The trip can be planned when it is much less crowded.

Children can learn how to do these things by modeling. In Islamic schools and Islamic weekend schools many teachers organize events to model Hajj. This could be done at home as well, but the community environment of many Muslims makes a better experience. Someone constructs a model of the Kabbah, the stone building in Mecca we all turn toward in salah, and models or posters of the different stages of Hajj. Teachers explain the story of Hajar (r) and Ibrahim (s) and their child Ismael (s). Children recite the talbiyah, a special chant recited during Hajj, as they walk around the Kabbah model. They pretend to throw stones at the station of Mina, a place near Mecca. In a group, they walk around the gym acting in the role of pilgrims. Teachers can make this as elaborate as they have time and ability. Some schools have a family night so children can share this experience with their parents. A Hajji (someone who has made Hajj) can tell stories of Hajj or Umrah to the children. And, of course, children should hear of different people they know who may undertake the journey. They will also join the family celebration when a family member returns from Hajj and hear those stories.

Modesty

The Prophet (s) said, "Iman [faith] has over seventy branches, and modesty is a branch of Iman." (Muslim, an-Nasa'i)

The Qur'an guides the way to one of the first ways parents teach modesty to their children:

All you who believe! Make your bonded servants and the young (children) among you ask your permission (before coming in a private room to see you) at these three times: before the pre-dawn prayer, when you've disrobed for an afternoon rest, and after the time of the late-night prayer has ended. These are the three times when (people are likely) to be undressed. Outside of these times, it isn't wrong for them to move around and interact with each other (in the home). This is how Allah clearly (explains) the verses to you, for Allah is full of knowledge and wisdom. After those young children among you reach puberty, they still must ask for permission, even as those older than they must, and (again) this is how Allah clearly (explains) His verses to you, for Allah is (indeed) full of knowledge and wisdom.. (Qur'an 24:58-59)

We start training children about modesty from when they are quite young by our example of how we dress and guard our modesty in front of them. Parents should create times for privacy from their children, so their children won't see them undressed. This gives parents some down time too, away from the stress of childcare.

As they grow, we push them to copy us. They should get dressed in their bedrooms and not parade around the house undressed. They need to dress properly before going outside. They also learn to shut the door to the bathroom when they are using it. They help close the curtains or blinds over the windows when it starts getting dark and people could see in. They learn to hold guests at the door before admitting them, so any women in the family have time to cover themselves.

Different cultures and different climates have slightly different rules on how to dress modestly. It is generally considered proper by Muslim scholars that everyone cover from the waist to the knee in any circumstance. Mothers can uncover their breasts to nurse their babies except when non-mahram men are present. (Mahram are men and boys of the family, those who could not marry a woman according to Qur'an.) Outside the home, from the age of puberty, girls and women should cover themselves in loose-fitting non-transparent clothes that only show their face and hands. How people apply the general rules varies considerably throughout the Muslim world.

We should encourage our children to wear clothes similar to what we wear, at least for special occasions. They will get comfortable with these clothes and learn to visualize themselves as adult-like when they wear them. Children also like to dress up in costumes and pretend that they are big. Dressing the part of an adult Muslim can help them be proud of their Muslim identity.

Let our daughters play with scarves and try them on. Let them play with different styles and colors to find out what they like. Some parents let their daughters wear scarves when they want and take them off when they want. Others set a rule. "If you decide to wear hijab to go shopping with Mom, wear it until you get home. Don't play around with it, taking it on and off at the store." These learning experiences will be different in different cultural environments. In some cultural groups, even little girls wear hijab outside all the time. In most groups, girls younger than puberty age only wear it for salah and maybe for going to the mosque and Islamic school classes.

In their worry to teach their daughters about hijab, some families forget that it is perfectly ok to dress up in beautiful clothes and makeup around family and with other girls. While the primary focus of girls should not be on looking beautiful, this aspect of life should not be discouraged.

Hodan and Nimo are sisters, just eighteen months apart in age, but very different from each other. Hodan loves dolls and kitty cats. She grew up spending lots of time dressing her dolls, herself, and trying to get the family cat to wear costumes. She loves to fuss with her hair and get her mother to braid it into different styles. Nimo only plays with dolls occasionally when her sister insists and there is nothing else to do. She rarely looks at herself in the mirror and will throw on mismatched clothes to run outside and play. Their mother frequently wonders why she can't shake the two girls up in a box and balance them out. She has to force Hodan to dress more quickly and stop fussing about her clothes. She also has to grab Nimo before she leaves the house and make sure she looks reasonably put together and has combed her hair. How many times has she gone to school with mismatched socks? Her mother is in despair. Their brother Abokar is just as bad as Nimo.

Nimo and Abokar will probably grow easily into adulthood and modest appropriate clothes. Hodan may be a problem. There is a place in the community for people with Hodan's eye for design and color. What we want to do is channel her sense of style into appropriate activities.

She will be very interested in learning what style of outfit is respectable for school or for play and may find a way to give the outfit a dash of fun within those guidelines. Let her help shop for her clothes and have some say. While Nimo may not notice clothes, Hodan can be very sensitive to how she looks and what people say about them. Let her enjoy planning and preparing for parties with girlfriends or dressing up with her mother to go to weddings. Her mother can discuss with her how we want to dress beautifully for the people we love, not for people in the street or the kids at school. Gradually her mother can test her in making her own decisions about her clothes, so she feels they are her style, but within her mother's guidelines she has adopted. There will likely be some arguments between Hodan and her mother. And Hodan may adopt a style different from her mother. But if her mom's goal is to get her to follow the same general guidelines for dress, there should be enough variation possible for both of them.

Boys need training in modesty as well. Though most boys clothing is loose fitting and comfortable for them, they need to cover to the knee so shorts can be a problem. There are swimming suits and some sports outfits that are very tight and not appropriate for our boys. And boys need to learn how to guard their eyes from looking at girls and women. Before the order in Qur'an for women to dress modestly is the order for men to lower their gaze.

Boys and men are particularly affected by visual images. That's why publicity uses alluringly dressed women in commercials to sell all kinds of items from cars to coffee. The order in Qur'an is for men to lower their gaze but that can be a problem in different cultures where looking down can be understood as weakness or hiding something and a person should demonstrate honesty and strength by looking at others straight in the eye. Though we want to train our boys to lower their gaze, we may have to talk about that as a figurative expression. Boys need to learn to look their female teachers and classmates straight in the eye at times. A tactful remark can help guide them in how to implement the Qur'an about this.

Disasters occur when parents let their children dress like all the kids at school and then spring it on them at puberty that they have to dress modestly. Their children are not prepared. They have identified with their friends at school and have never imagined dressing differently. If a parent is in this position, for whatever reason, it's better not to insist on the issue. Children at puberty are now adult enough to make their own decisions about their clothes and their behavior. At this age, we can only explain why they should dress modestly and encourage them, but we have to let them take their time and make their own choices. We may control the money, but young people have ways of taking off scarves and borrowing make-up from friends and other ways of changing their dress once away from parent's eyes. It is very sad when children lead double lives, one at home and the mosque and a second very different life at school and off with friends.

School often creates problems for parents. Public schools may require sports outfits that are skimpy, for boys as well as girls. Some teachers may exert pressure on children to wear short shorts. A particular problem may be the school locker rooms, where middle school or high school children are expected to change and shower in front of each other.

Other parents are a good source of information about how the school handles these issues. How bad is the problem? In the United States, schools are required to make accommodation for religion and special needs, so there is often a solution ready with the teacher or principal whenever someone asks. But teachers sometimes think a student who asks for a favor is out of line so parental involvement may be necessary, even if it embarrasses the student. (Many teens are hypersensitive about embarrassment.)

One family found their son could take the required gym class during summer school, when he could wear his gym clothes to school for the class and return home to shower. A girl got permission to change in a larger bathroom for special needs, which had a shower. The family might join with other parents, Muslim, special needs, and others, and pressure the school to renovate the locker rooms to create many private change and shower areas.

4 - TEACHING DESIRED BEHAVIOR

In addition to modeling how to do things with our children, we also have to consider how we talk to our children, to explain things to them, and how we control or set up the environment for them.

Prophet Muhammad (s) had the task of teaching a whole population of people of all sorts of backgrounds and levels of education and he did it so well that people were able to pass on his teachings, and the message he brought, in a clear accurate manner that came down to us today. So looking at how he taught, as illuminated in hadith, provides us with an excellent example of a teacher with an enduring legacy.

Prophet Muhammad had to establish rapport with the people so that they would listen to him. People respected him and cared about him. They felt he had something valuable to tell them so they memorized his words. They noticed his face, if he looked upset or pleased, and they described his reactions in hadith.

This rapport didn't happen overnight. If we read the story of the prophet's life, we see how long it took for him to establish himself and convince people of his role as prophet. At first, only his close family listened and believed in him, along with a few close friends. Early followers often had to hide their faith and they were persecuted.

But the prophet treated people so well, with modesty and good manners, that he impressed them. Khadijah (r), a wealthy widow, was so impressed with his services to her and his good manners and morals that she married him and was the first to believe in him.

His adopted son Zayd bin Haritha had been a slave of Khadijah's. When Prophet Muhammad (s) came to live with her, she gave him Zayd to be his servant. Then Zayd's father came to town and offered to pay for the boy's freedom. But Zayd was so happy where he was that he chose to stay in slavery there, serving this kind man. Hearing his choice, Prophet Muhammad (s) freed Zayd and adopted him. Zayd (r) was among the first converts to Islam after Khadijah (r).

Many adults seem to feel that rapport with children isn't important. They treat their bosses and adults they feel are socially important with all respect and curtesy, but inside the house "no one" will notice and they do and say whatever they want. Children and servants, and often their own friends, don't count to receive their best behavior. Also, behind the closed doors of their home, people feel they can vent their anger and frustration with whatever is happening outside, often yelling at their children because they are just tired after a long day at work or upset with a financial problem. But this is not Islamic behavior. Allah notices even if the door is closed to the outside world, and the recording angels are doing their job. We should always use our best behavior, especially with those we love.

The Best Language

Prophet Muhammad spoke well to everyone, including to children. His servant boy Anas bin Malik (r) recounted:

"The Messenger of Allah (s) was one of the best of men in character. One day he sent me to do something, and I said, "I swear by Allah that I will not go." But in my heart I felt that I should go to do what the Prophet of Allah (s) had commanded me; so I went out and came upon some boys who were playing in the street. All of a sudden the Messenger of Allah (s), who had come up behind, caught me by the back of the neck, and when I looked at him he was laughing. He said, "Go where I ordered you, little Anas." I replied, "Yes, I am going, Messenger of Allah!"" Anas said, "I swear by Allah, I served him for seven or nine years, and he never said to me about a thing which I had done, 'Why did you do such and such?' Nor about a thing which I left, 'why did you not do such and such?'" (Abu Dawud, Muslim)

Other hadith narrators remembered their childhood:

Narrated the uncle of Abu Rafi ibn Amr al-Ghifari (r), "I was a boy. I used to throw stones at the palm-trees of the Ansar. So I was brought to the Prophet (s) who said, "Oh boy, why do you throw stones at the palm trees?" I said, "To eat (dates)." He said "Do not throw stones at the palm trees, but eat what falls beneath them." He then wiped the child's head and said, "Oh Allah, fill his belly.""" (Abu Dawud, Ibn Majah)

Narrated Umar bin Abi Salama (r), "I was a boy under the care of Allah's Messenger (s) and my hand used to go around the dish while I was eating. So Allah's Messenger (s) said to me, "Oh boy! Mention the Name of Allah and eat with your right hand, and eat of the food what is nearer to you." Since then I have applied those instructions when eating." (Bukhari)

He even ordered people to correct their language when talking to inanimate things.

Once in the time of the Prophet (s), the wind snatched away a man's cloak and he cursed the wind. The Prophet (s) said, "Do not curse it, for it is under (Allah's) command, and if anyone curses a thing undeservedly, the curse returns upon him." (Abu Dawud)

Shouldn't we use our best language and manners with those we love the most? In Islam, our manners and moral character are not supposed to be an image we project outside, hiding an inner person who is mean and angry. Following Islamic behavior should be an all-the-time experience. At first the behavior might seem awkward, but over time and with effort, we absorb it and become better people. Allah (swt) rewards us for our efforts to improve. The mean ideas and anger gradually disappear.

Don't damage each other's reputations nor be sarcastic with each other, and don't call each other by (cruel) nicknames. It's terrible to use an insulting nickname for someone after he's become a believer. Whoever doesn't stop this practice is doing wrong. (Qur'an 49:11)

Invite (others) to the way of your Lord with wisdom and beautiful preaching, and reason with them in ways that are best. Your lord knows best who is straying from His path and who is being guided (towards it). (Qur'an 16:125)

Abu Abdullah Al-Jadali narrated, "I asked Aisha about the character of the Messenger of Allah. She said, 'He was not obscene, nor uttering obscenities, nor screaming in the markets. He would not return an evil with an evil, but rather he was pardoning and forgiving." (Tirmidhi)

Abdullah bin Amr (r) said, The Messenger of Allah (s) neither talked in an insulting manner nor did he ever speak evil intentionally. He used to say, "The best among you is the one who has the best manners and character." (Bukhari)

The prophet spoke in a few well-chosen words that were easy to remember. He was known for his good, high-quality, polite language. One of the ways scholars qualify hadith is by the words used and how they are put together. The prophet had a memorable style. It was terse, using just a few words to express his ideas.

Aisha reported, ""The Messenger of Allah (s) did not speak quickly like you do now, rather he would speak so clearly, unmistakably, that those who sat with him would memorize it." (Tirmidhi)

Prophet Muhammad (s) chose his time to speak. He wasn't always going around giving speeches and advice and pushing himself on others. He deliberately gave people space and waited for the right moment to speak. Abdullah ibn Abbas (r), told people what he had learned from Prophet Muhammad:

"Preach to the people once a week, and if you want, then preach them twice, but if you want to preach more, then let it be three times (a week only), and do not make the people fed-up with this Qur'an. If you come to some people who are engaged in a talk, don't start interrupting their talk by preaching, or you might cause them to be bored. You should rather keep quiet, and if they ask you, then preach to them at the time when they are eager to hear what you say. And avoid the use of rhymed prose in invocation for I noticed that Allah's Messenger (s) and his companions always avoided it." (Bukhari)

There are many hadith that show the Prophet asking permission to speak to someone before giving advice, including his own daughter.

Narrated Ali bin Abi Talib: Fatima came to the Prophet (s) asking for a servant. He said, "May I inform you of something better than that? When you go to bed, recite "Subhan Allah' thirty three times, 'Alhamdulillah' thirty three times, and 'Allahu Akbar' thirty four times. Ali added, 'I have never failed to recite it ever since." (Bukhari)

Many hadith show the Prophet waited for others to ask him questions before speaking.

Sufyan bin Abdullah ath-Thaqafee (r) said, "Oh Messenger of Allah, tell me something about Islam which I can ask of no one but you." He (s) said, "Say I believe in Allah - and then be steadfast." (Muslim)

So how do we instruct our children? Prophet Muhammad knew his people and listened to them. Parents too need to listen to a child's feelings, fears, and hopes. Many parents and teachers lecture on and on without pausing to notice if the child is listening and understands. If he or she isn't or doesn't, they decide it's the child's fault for not accepting their valuable efforts to teach. But teaching is a two-way street.

When Sam wants to instruct his small child about how to cross the street, first he has to get the child's attention and permission to talk. With a young child, this means using words the child understands and often showing him concretely, while on the side of the street, when the child is ready to start across it.

Sam holds Lana's hand. "Ok Lana, look both ways. Turn your head both ways to see if there are any cars. Are there any?" Sam observes Lana turn her head to check the street. Lana, "No Daddy." "So can we cross the street?" Lana looks up at Sam with worry. "Yes Lana, now we can cross," he reassures her. By following this routine several times, Lana will become confident to answer. Then slowly Sam can let go of her hand and let her tell him when to cross. When she has mastered it, he will let her cross on her own while he watches her. He will know, by watching, how well she has learned and how much she can do on her own.

A wise parent teaches in stages, according to the child's ability and understanding. Children have short attention spans so keeping lessons brief and the project simple leads to a better outcome. As they grow, we can increase the complexity and time needed to complete the task.

To learn to clean a room, picking up is a good starting point. It's useful to have a box for toys and maybe a shelf where things can be set. The goal is to get stuff off the floor. With younger children, we don't expect them to line things up neatly, though some will. Model the task for the child first, then gradually encourage him to do it all by himself. "My, what a big boy!" Some children take more time than others to learn to store things neatly rather than in a bunch. A young child might play with the vacuum but it takes a much older child to have the strength and understanding to move the vacuum in an organized pattern around the floor. "Oh, the air smells so much fresher when the room is all clean!"

With many school age children, focusing on the speed they work can increase their proficiency at tasks. Bilal times his children for how long it takes them to get dressed in the morning. They love to hear the excitement he puts into his race car announcer voice when he stands in the hall and yells that the morning race is ready to begin. He calls out each child's name as they jump out of bed. "Susu has crossed the starting line with Mimi following in close pursuit!" They love to run up to him and look at his phone to see the time as he calls out the minutes and seconds. The energy gets everyone fully awake and ready for salah and breakfast with minimal effort from Bilal. He just stands there with his phone and yells out the time while the children run around finding all their clothes and getting dressed. If he records each child's time, he can compare that time to the time the child took yesterday rather than comparing the children to each other. Reducing competition and comparing a child to her own track record lowers the sense of one child being preferred over another, something we don't want to do.

Controlling the Environment

One of the qualities of a good teacher is to create a safe environment for children where they can feel free and interested in learning. In the beginning of his mission, Prophet Muhammad (s) could not do much to create a supportive environment for the new Muslim community. But as the group grew, he was able to send some of them to Abyssinia, where, under the Christian ruler, they could practice their faith in relative peace. Later he looked for a town that would take in his followers and arranged for the Muslims to emigrate to Yathrib (Medina). He engaged with anyone who was willing to talk with him, explaining the faith, looking for new converts, but also working to help people understand Islam and allow the Muslims to worship in peace as much as he could.

Under the section Financial Responsibility, in Chapter 2, the home environment and the choice of caretakers for the child were discussed. This is an important part of controlling the environment.

Whatever space we have to live in, we can also try to arrange it to be child-friendly. Keeping things neat and organized helps, especially in smaller spaces. Work to arrange for the children to eat regular meals and get peaceful sleep. This is important for their health and also for them to feel comfortable and ready to learn, either in school or in living with family.

If children have to switch houses between their divorced parents, try to make these moves as stress-free as possible. Divorced parents should try not to argue or fight in front of the children. The best situation is to follow the advice of the Qur'an, 2:233 which says parents should consult with each other and be reasonable so neither is treated unfairly.

The best situation doesn't always occur. The divorced parents may hate each other and have little respect for each other. But their child loves both of them—and should be allowed the right to do this. If we reflect on all the importance Qur'an gives to the parents, and the respect a person should show to his or her parents, it is very arrogant to work to make a child fear or hate a parent. If we can't say something good about the parent, it is better to say nothing to a young child. When a child is older and can handle the truth, we can tactfully discuss issues. It's very important to remember the rules on talking about other people, no backbiting and no slander.

All you who believe! Don't let some men among you make fun of other men, for it may be that the (ones who are being made fun of) are better than the (ones making fun of them). And don't let some women (make fun of) other women, either for it may be that the (ones being made fun of) are better than the (ones who are making fun of them). Don't damage each other's reputations nor be sarcastic with each other, and don't call each other by (cruel) nicknames. It's terrible to use an insulting nickname for someone after he's become a believer. Whoever doesn't stop this practice is doing wrong. All you who believe! Avoid being overly suspicious (of your fellow believers) for suspicion in some cases is a sin. Don't spy on each other nor speak

badly about each other behind their backs. Would any of you like to eat the flesh of his dead brother? (Qur'an 49:11-12)

"Do you know what is backbiting?" They (the Companions) said, "Allah and His Messenger know best." Thereupon he (the Holy Prophet) said, "Backbiting implies your talking about your brother in a manner which he does not like." It was said to him, "What is your opinion about this that if I actually find (that failing) in my brother which I made a mention of?" He said, "If (that failing) is actually found (in him) what you assert, you in fact backbit him, and if that is not in him, it is a slander." (Muslim)

Sandy divorced Hoissein because he refused to support her and the children. He does see the children off and on and takes them out for a good time. Sandy feels resentful of his visits as well as of his lack of financial contribution. If Sandy keeps her hurt to herself, avoiding backbiting and slandering her ex, the kids can love to see Daddy and look forward to his rare visits. Children don't understand finances. They will absorb here and there some of the truth about why there isn't enough money for the things they want or need as they grow, but Sandy doesn't need to make it a major issue for them. It's hard. He takes them out for one afternoon of fun while she has all the work of raising them plus paying all the bills. The children will grow to understand the difference eventually.

People are complex. There is good and bad in everyone. Older children can understand and process that. Younger children tend to see the world in black and white. If the young child learns his father (or mother) is horrible, then Daddy (or Mommy) is all bad. The child can have a hard time forming a positive ideal image of a parent that all children need. And the child can feel badly about himself or herself. "How can I be a good person, or parent, someday when I come from someone who was bad?"

There is a time in adolescence when children are thinking about how they are going to be as adults. This is the time they become critical of their parents and start planning their own path. They have formed an ideal of what a parent should be inside their minds and they can understand how their real parents are different from those ideals. This is a better time for them to learn of the problems their parents have had in life and the poor or difficult decisions they may have made, if they need to hear them. And all discussions should be conducted using Islamic guidelines for speech.

There are situations when children must know a horrible truth about a parent. Maybe the parent is in prison for selling drugs or stealing. Maybe the child was conceived following a rape. Maybe the children live with their father because their mother ran off with another man. Whatever the problem, we want to raise the innocent child in the best way, so that the child can grow up to be a strong healthy adult and be a good parent when the time comes for that someday. We tell them the minimum facts necessary at the time when the subject comes up and we try very hard not to be judgmental in our discussion. The child is a good person and loved. Hopefully there will be good role models around for them, adults from extended family who can fill in for the missing parent.

Having good playmates is probably more important than toys for children of all ages. It is worth it for parents to work on developing friendships with other parents just so their children can have good friends. We need to consider the moral character of the children our children play with as they grow older. We need to plan trips to parks and recreation facilities with good friends. We need to cross town if necessary to allow our children to have good friends.

A man follows the religion of his friend; so each one should consider who he makes his friend. (Abu Dawud, Tirmidhi)

When children are small, we can shield them from undesirable friends and games. Screen time can be strictly limited. Apps for the electronic tablet and video games can be checked out before our children use them. As children grow and get out in the community more, we can shield them less and less. We need to train them to develop their own shields. If they are used to people being polite and well-mannered around them, they will look for friends who are like that too and screen out the rude ones. They will feel uncomfortable with coarse, mean games and videos and look for something better.

Another part of controlling the environment is to adopt rules of manners that encourage respect. Here we are reflecting back on the topic of adab from Chapter 3. Implementing adab will have the effect of organizing the environment of the home and family in a positive manner. There are rules that are mentioned in Qur'an and hadith. People in the different regions of the world where Islam has spread have put these rules into practice, often adding their own details. In new cultural environments where Islam is being introduced, parents will adapt these rules again and decide how flexible they want or need to be. It's easier if there is a community that is in agreement, that creates a community standard of behavior.

One example of this system of adab will be presented here. In Islam, it's important to respect those who are older and those who are guests in the house. In some Muslim cultures, they extend this concept to giving titles to older brothers and sisters, like "agabey" for older brother and "abla" for older sister in Turkish, along with the titles "aunt" and "grandpa" etc. It is also common to require younger brothers and sisters to yield to older ones, particularly when there is a big age difference. This is part of showing respect for others, regardless of their personal merit. We are not left with the option of deciding for ourselves whether to respect someone or not.

Anas bin Malik narrated that, "An older man came to talk to the Prophet, and the people were hesitant to make room for him. The Prophet said, "He is not one of us who does not have mercy on our young and does not respect our elders."" (Tirmidhi)

Joe is serving fruit salad to both company and the whole family. His children, Fatima, age eight, and Sami, age six, both arrive at the serving table at the same time calling out "Me!" and reaching a hand out for a bowl. In many places, good manners require that Joe make sure the company has been served first, maybe asking the children to help handing out the fruit bowls. Then they need to make sure older family members get their servings. Then maybe because Fatima is older she might get hers before her brother, but they are close in age so maybe not. This is a formal setting and the children are witnessing how Joe gives everyone his or her due. In a more informal setting, at the ice cream shop, Sami might get his first because he is standing closest to Joe or he decided his order first. There are other, just as arbitrary ways to decide who gets something first.

Another practice of adab is to pass things around when in a group, always in the same direction. This way everyone gets a turn and the one initiating the sharing is saved from worrying about which way to start. (This habit is also used when asking people to contribute to a discussion. Someone can pass if he or she doesn't want to speak, but everyone in attendance gets to contribute without having to raise a hand and depend on the leader to notice.)

Narrated Sahl bin Sa`d, "Allah's Messenger (s) was offered something to drink. He drank of it while on his right was a boy and on his left were some elderly people. He said to the boy, "May I give these (elderly) people first?" The boy said, "By Allah, Oh Allah's Messenger (s)! I will not give up my share from you to somebody else." On that Allah's Messenger (s) placed the cup in the hand of that boy. "(Bukhari, Muslim)

In this hadith we see the Prophet (s) balancing different practices, a custom of passing food or drink to the right around a group with the custom of serving the elders first. We notice his gentle treatment of the boy, asking him which rule to follow. The child chose to go first. Receiving his turn directly from the Prophet was very important for him. And the Prophet respected his choice. This shows us the flexibility of these practices and how the Prophet (s) respected the child.

If Joe, from the example above, was seated at a table with his guests and family, following this second rule of adab, he would have served the fruit bowls and passed them to his right around the table until everyone was served.

Parents also need to balance several considerations when deciding among their children. Some children have special needs, a disability or an illness, that may mean they get preference. A girl may get her own bedroom while her brothers have to share a room. Having a system of manners and rules of consideration that are known to all in the family, that respect each member of the family, help us create an environment where everyone feels more comfortable.

Moderation

A good teacher knows the level of his or her students and asks them to do things that are not too hard, yet not too easy. Since children are growing in ability and knowledge all the time, teachers need to continually adjust the level of their lessons.

Remember the story of the ascent of Prophet Muhammad (s) to Paradise and his conversation with Prophet Musa (s). They were concerned that Allah was asking the people to do more prayers than they could accomplish. Prophet Musa advised Prophet Muhammad (peace and blessings on them both) to go ask for reductions. And we have many hadith that show Prophet Muhammad's concern for causing hardship to his people by demanding too much of them.

"Religion is very easy and whoever overburdens himself in his religion will not be able to continue in that way. So you should not be extremists, but try to be near to perfection and receive the good tidings that you will be rewarded; and gain strength by worshipping in the mornings, the afternoons, and during the last hours of the nights." (Bukhari)

"If it were not that it would be difficult on my nation, then I would have ordered them to use miswak [a natural toothbrush] before each prayer." (Bukhari, Tirmidhi)

A bedouin urinated in the mosque and the people ran to (beat) him. Allah's Messenger (s) said, "Do not interrupt his urination (i.e. let him finish)." Then the Prophet (s) asked for a tumbler of water and poured the water over the place of urine. (Bukhari)

A man from Najd with unkempt hair came to the Messenger of Allah (s). He was speaking loudly but his speech could not be understood until he came close. He was asking about Islam. The Messenger of Allah (s) said, "Five prayers every day and night." He said, "Do I have to do any more than that?" He said, "No, not unless you do it voluntarily." The Messenger of Allah (s) said, "Fasting the month of Ramadan." He said, "Do I have to do any more than that?" He said, "No, not unless you do it voluntarily." Then the Messenger of Allah (s) told him about zakah. He said, "Do I have to do any more than that?' He said, "No, not unless you do it voluntarily." The man left saying, 'I will not do any more than that or any less." The Messenger of Allah (s) said, "He will succeed, if he is telling the truth." (Tirmidhi)

113

An example of structuring things for ease can be found in teaching the memorization of Qur'an. We may challenge our children to continually learn new surahs (chapters) of Qur'an. We hear of children who have memorized the whole Qur'an by age 7 or 8. But each child has a different ability to memorize and we can tailor the lessons and the rate of progress to suit each child's ability.

One child may memorize easily and start picking up ayahs (verses) when listening to recitation during salah. This child may memorize whole parts by listening to audio recordings that he or she can play alone on their own audio equipment. Young children who haven't learned to read may also profit from this method.

Most children learn to memorize Qur'an while they are learning to read Arabic. This method has advantages because children can see where one word begins and another ends. They can be taught the vocabulary and grammar along with their memorization efforts and learn to understand what they are reciting. Like learning to read in English, children vary a great deal in their ability to decode and comprehend writing. Some read fluently by the age of 4. But the developing brain may not be wired properly until the age of 9. Parents and teachers need to exercise patience with children and allow them time to grow and learn at their own rate.

And there are many children with learning disabilities that cause them to be poor readers without specialized teaching. An Arabic class that focuses on teaching spoken Arabic is necessary to teach these children to understand the Qur'an they recite, and the first method of memorizing from hearing works best for them.

For older students, who didn't have the chance to learn to read Arabic but want to learn Qur'an, there are phonetic texts available using English script to support their learning. Insha Allah, (if Allah wills) they will learn to read Arabic with time, but these texts can help them start the salah (formal prayers) more quickly.

Communication Without Taboos

As a teacher of all subjects of Islam, Prophet Muhammad (s) was not shy to discuss a wide array of topics with his companions. Upon the request of the women of the community, he arranged one day a week for them to have full access to his teachings, so they could ask any questions without being bothered by men in attendance. He also encouraged his wives to discuss intimate issues privately with women. The Muslim community understood the importance of these topics so they passed down hadith on such issues as using the bathroom, how to do ghusl (total body wash for purification), wet dreams and menstruation, and sexual relations between men and women, among many other topics. As parents, we too need to address these topics with our children and pass down the information.

The Islamic ideal of marriage needs to be explained to the Muslim child. Children need to know early, well before the dating age, how we expect them to find a mate in life, and how we will help them. Tell them how Mommy and Daddy met and how other friends and family members found spouses. Let them come to any weddings that allow children and participate in the parties in any way they can.

Traditionally, Muslims married people from their neighborhood or village, in a social environment where everyone already knew everyone. The reputations of people were well known and arranged marriages were relatively safe. They were also unions of families as much as unions of couples. Both families were joined by marriage. With the extended social networks people had, through family and friends, marriages were not relied on to supply so much of a person's social engagement. When women attend social functions for women, their marital status isn't important. They go with mothers and sisters, with their children and cousins. It's the same for men. This takes a lot of pressure off the couple.

Today, the marriage is central to the identity of a couple. Couples do things together and are invited to events together. They need a great deal of compatibility in this environment because they spend a lot of time together and have few other important social relationships. In this context, it is essential that a potential couple get to know each other well before getting married. The Muslim community is adapting to this change, allowing a lot more freedom for potential couples to meet, and letting people take a lot more time to decide whether to marry or not.

Our children are growing up in an environment where boys and girls are expected to learn and play in mixed gender groups. Often the children grow up and have no particular attraction to each other in these groups, or attraction occurs for only short periods and quickly fades.

There is a problem with economic maturity being very different from biological maturity. That means, people grow to be adults, physically able to marry and have children, long before their education is finished and they have the financial means to support a family. The non-Muslim society is handling this today by focusing pressure on education and careers rather than on marriage for both boys and girls. Then it tacitly accepts that young adults will be sexually active in one way or another.

Of course, for a Muslim, any sexual activity outside of marriage is haram (forbidden) so our young adults are placed in an awkward position. With most children, parents can encourage education and career, and promise that when the time is right, they will help their children get married to someone wonderful. Just wait! However, some young people feel the sexual urge too strongly, or their career options aren't very compelling to overcome the attraction to marriage. If a young person really wants marriage, we should help them rather than have them do something outside of marriage. It is harder to earn a college degree or career training after marriage, but it is possible, particularly if parents continue their financial assistance and moral support.

By puberty, a Muslim youngster will be aware that many non-Muslim children are having a difficult time because of the heavy emphasis on having relations with the opposite sex. Because of the early age at which non-Muslim children start such relationships, and the prominence of talk about sex in American culture as a whole, we need to discuss such matters with our children early, probably well before sixth grade. Parents can ask other parents with older children for advice concerning the local situation.

It would probably be helpful to just tell children up front. Part of the changes of growing into a man or woman include the awareness of sexual attraction. This is a normal feeling in adults that children don't have. It is independent of feelings of friendship or even knowing the other person. We can feel sexual attraction to a picture or a complete stranger we pass on the street. It is mostly visual, and it can complicate the lives of adults. Muslims have a system for minimizing these feelings in public. We lower our gaze and dress modestly. We try to stay out of situations where a man

116

and a woman are too close and their feelings of attraction can lead them to act inappropriately. These feelings can overwhelm a person and make them do silly things, like showing off or acting awkwardly or very shy. Allah gave us these feelings so that we can find someone to marry but that means they should be channeled into the right social setting when we are seriously considering marriage. In other situations, they just cause all kinds of problems.

Young people must learn how to manage these feelings. We teach them to control their hunger and they learn to fast. We teach them to control their tongues and they learn to be polite and tactful. This new challenge is similar. Kids worry so much about how they look and what others might be saying about them because they want to have friends. Then around puberty, this feeling of sexual attraction is added to the mix and they feel even more discomfort. Kids tell inappropriate jokes or boast to cover their insecurities about dating and attracting members of the opposite sex. In such an environment, Muslim youth need support in realizing that their feelings of shyness are normal and that, although no one admits it much, these feelings are experienced by most of their non-Muslim classmates as well. As they get older, everyone gets used to these feelings and learns ways to control them.

In addition to feelings of sexual attraction, normal adults have sexual needs that vary in strength over their lifetimes. Satisfying these needs can be very pleasurable and satisfying, or full of pain and heartache. Allah has guided us to look to our partners in marriage to satisfy these needs. Looking elsewhere is where the pain and heartache come. And the Qur'an has told us about our spouses:

They're like a garment for you and you're like a garment for them. (Qur'an 2:187)

We want marriage partners who, like a garment, beautify us, make us comfortable, and protect us through the years.

And among His signs is the fact that He created spouses for you from among your own kind so you can dwell with them in harmony. Indeed, He put love and mercy between you, and there are signs in this for people who think. (Qur'an 30:21)

117

With all the divorces around us and people living together without marriage in our communities, we need to be very clear about the beautiful goals we have in seeking marriage and how much we want these blessings for our children.

Managing menstruation, pregnancy, wet dreams and other topics may be best handled in a class about taharah, (ritual purity or cleanliness) at the mosque or Islamic school. How people have babies should also be covered. There the topics can be handled in single sex groups with sensitive teachers. (The quality and training of the teacher are very important.) Teaching these topics in general should ensure that young people get a full clear understanding. Parents don't often have the material available to them and the relationship between child and parent can interfere. Classroom settings generally cover topics more widely, bringing up details that parents and children don't think of in discussions at home. They can also include the topics of food purity and not misusing drugs and other chemicals in our bodies. It's very important to put all these topics into the context of personal purity and Islamic worship.

That doesn't mean parents can just drop their children off at the mosque school and ignore sex education completely. Short conversations at home are important. Parents usually cover a topic quickly when it comes up, without much overview or detail.

Hazem noticed his older daughter slipping a sanitary napkin to his younger daughter who just started her period a few months ago. The younger girl darted away toward the bathroom. Later when he calls the prayer for maghrib, his younger daughter comes running to put on her clothes for salah. He leans over to whisper to her sister, "Should Jasmine be praying now?" His older daughter straightens her prayer scarf and then goes to whisper to Jasmine. Jasmine quickly folds her prayer things and slips to the back of the room as her mother enters. Hazem mentions the issue to his wife after the salah and she goes to have a quick chat with Jasmine. She might do a little du'a with Jasmine, thanking Allah for the ease He gives them not to require salah during their periods and asking for good health. The boys of the family don't even notice anything happened.

Sajda notices semen on her son's pajamas as she is preparing to do the wash. She calls on him to join her and privately shows them to him. "When this happens, you need to change your clothes and do ghusl (bath of purification) before you pray, Dear. "What is that stuff Mom?" he asks. "You've had a wet dream, Jamaal. It's a normal part of growing up to be a man. Just go, wash, and put on clean clothes before you go to pray any time you notice this."

Seven-year-old Arif just heard his aunt is going to have a fourth child and he is getting a new cousin. He announces loudly to the family group, "Wow, she got married 4 times then." Everyone laughs and ignores him. A bit later his father takes him aside and asks him why he thinks his aunt got married 4 times. Arif responds that you need to get married to have a baby, and she is going to have another baby. His father gently clarifies that his aunt only got married once, and the idea is that you need to be married before you have any children, but once you are married you can have any number of children. Now Arif knows why people laughed. Keeping the conversation respectful and easy between father and son should encourage Arif to come to his father if he has any more questions.

What about the neighbor girl who is pregnant? She lives with her parents and doesn't seem to have a husband? It is possible for someone to have a baby without getting married, but that is very sad. Allah told us not to do that. The baby won't have both his parents there to raise him and Allah wants each baby to have a mother and father. It's possible to manage with a parent missing but it is very hard and Allah wants us to seek the best way to live, in loving families who support us and help us.

Open communication with our children is very important and parents need to be well informed about the world "out there" where they are sending their children each day. The modern world changes quickly and the worries we had as children ourselves may be out of date.

In the difficult age we live in, a parents' support group, however informal, is a real benefit. Find out what is really going on at school, beyond stereotypes. Some parents can volunteer at school activities and inform others who can't. Some parents communicate better with school staff, or are members of school staff. Some are good at talking with their kids. If parents can network and learn what is really going on in school, they are more likely to be able to communicate with their children in a constructive way. One story of a school shooting three states away or drugs being found in a student's locker across town can make a parent's imagination run out of control with worry.

Generally, schools are much less dangerous than the news implies. With a pool of several hundred students, our children may well be hanging out with a few nice kids they found and be ignorant of the drug sale occurring right in front of them in the hall. But they could also have selected some of the wrong friends and hide things from their parents. Having friendships with other parents at the school can be a big help to parents. The parents can keep each other updated on events at school and support each other on any issues of concern.

Satan tempts people into doing wrong things. Then he continues to hold them by whispering that Allah will not forgive them. He works through people, often through friends. So a young person may feel pressure from them to do something he knows is wrong, or he may get excited and rationalize to himself and join in their wrongdoing. A bully may threaten him or blackmail him to keep him stuck in a gang or prevent him from telling adults who can stop the wrong doing and punish the wrong-doers.

We need to love our children as Allah loves us. Our children need to know that they can always turn to us for help. There may be some serious consequences for a bad deed and some requirement to make things right if possible, but there is always forgiveness and mercy, too. By definition we are not born in sin. We are born in fitra, pure. We are capable of both good and bad. The bad can be separated from the individual and condemned and dealt with. That's what purification is all about.

The best response is to remain loving and open, not tolerating or allowing an errant young person's misbehavior but trying to affect him or her by love, and not closing our hearts or our home to our child. Is it not an article of faith that Allah forgives all sins? As we forgive others, in spite of the personal hurt and harm they may have done to us, Allah will forgive us and them.

Sometimes we will need to engage outside help, experts in any given field. Addiction issues are very hard to overcome. Some kinds of mental illness like bipolar disorder or personality disorders can manifest themselves in the teen or early adult years. And some parents have difficulty drawing lines between helping and enabling, and err into enabling. The tremendous weapon we have, which is more powerful than any misbehavior or wrong doing, is prayer, for Allah surely responds to the prayer of a parent for a child.

And seek help through patience and prayer, though it isn't easy, except for the truly humble—those who realize that they're going to meet their lord and that they will return to Him. (Qur'an 2:45-46)

There are three prayers that will undoubtedly be answered: the prayer of one who has been wronged; the prayer of the traveler; and the prayer of a parent for his child. (Ibn Majah, Abu Dawud)

All you who believe! There are potential adversaries for you among your spouses and children, so watch out! However, if you overlook (their faults), gloss over (their shortcomings) and forgive them, (know that) Allah is forgiving and merciful. Your wealth and your children may be a test for you, but the greatest reward is in Allah's presence! (Qur'an 64:15)

"Be moderate and stand firm in trouble that falls to the lot of a Muslim (as that) removes sins from him; even stumbling on the path or the pricking of a thorn." (Muslim)

Kausar started using illegal soft drugs when she was 12. She would use the drugs at her girlfriend's house. Along with a group of friends, she tried opioids the kids stole from medicine cabinets and bought from other kids at school. She was able to hide her growing addiction problem from her parents, who were both busy working and focused on their marital problems.

She prayed with the family and did her homework and chores. Her grades slipped as she transitioned to high school but her parents thought that was because of the school change. She promised to study harder and they tried to give her more time at the public library to study, not knowing she would leave there as soon as she was dropped off, to go join her friends.

121

Some cash did disappear from her mom's purse sometimes but her mother didn't keep careful records of what she spent so she didn't catch on.

But when Kausar was 15 her mother finally caught on. By then she was shooting heroin. Kausar has a serious addiction problem. It is both medical and psychological. It would have been nice if her parents could have caught the problem back when she was 12 or 13, before the addiction took hold, but that is long past. Kausar needs addiction treatment.

Her parents need a lot of information about treatment options and how to treat their daughter in a way that helps her overcome her problem. They need a support network of understanding friends, too. We should not point fingers and try to blame the parents for the problem. That isn't helpful. Allah knows what the real cause was, or the multiple little errors in communication that occurred, that led to this. This is a big test for the whole family and will require all the strength and perseverance the parents can manage to help their daughter back to health. An important part of success will involve finding a place in society for Kausar with good people away from those who engage in drug cultural activities.

5 - REWARDING POSITIVE BEHAVIOR

This is a short chapter, not because rewards are not important, but rather because Chapter 2 has covered the topic of treating children with equity, which relates to how we reward them to be fair and avoid provoking jealousy. Here we explore ways to be thoughtful about how we reward them and how to encourage them to seek rewards from Allah (swt)

Allah rewards us and encourages us to search for His reward. He is also very generous with his rewards. Parents should visualize the 10 to 1 ratio of Allah (swt) when trying to find a balance between rewards and punishments with our children:

Whoever does something good will be given ten times as much to his credit, while whoever does an evil thing will be credited with one bad deed, and no one will ever be treated unfairly. (Qur'an 6:160)

It's not just the success of doing something that Allah rewards. He also rewards for intentions:

Allah says, (addressing the angels), "If My servant intends to do a bad deed, do not write it down unless he does it. If he does it, then write it down as it is. But if he refrains from doing it for My sake, then write it as a good deed. If he intends to do a good deed but does not do it, write a good deed (in his account), and if he does it, then write it for him as ten good deeds up to seven hundred times." (Bukhari, Muslim)

We need to have accountability in our homes and children need to know that punishment does happen and does exist, but this should be a minor part of life in an environment that is generally positive and encouraging with little rewards all around.

Rewards don't have to be big items, and we don't need to do high-fives throughout the day, but we should be encouraging the children to do good things, to do them well, and to feel comfortable with their efforts, even if they aren't successful. Our homes should be calm places where we can

123

spend some time playing, some time relaxing, some time doing chores and homework, and some time doing salah and remembering Allah. We look for moderation in all things.

All you who believe! Don't forbid the good things that Allah has allowed you. Just don't overindulge (in lawful things), for Allah has no love for the overindulgent. (Qur'an 5:87)

The Prophet's daughter Fatima (r), when she was grown and married, asked him if he could help her get a servant to help her with the work in her home. This was when he was finally being widely recognized as a prophet and people were donating considerable wealth to him which he was distributing widely among all the Muslim community. Many people had received much more than what she asked for. His reply is an example for us:

"Shall I not tell you of a thing which is better for you than a servant? When you (both) go to your beds, say 'Allahu Akbar' thirty-four times, and 'Subhan Allah' thirty-three times, 'Alhamdulillah' thirty-three times, for that is better for you than a servant." (Bukhari, Muslim)

We reward children with our approval, "Good job", with our interest in their work, "Tell me about this structure you built", and with our thanks, "I really appreciate how nicely you helped your little brother wash his hands."

Rewarding a child with too much praise can backfire. It can prevent the child from having a realistic idea about his or her ability. It can prevent a child from trying harder next time, because this time was already successful. Praising a child in front of others can also cause problems, like jealousy from other children.

A man praised another man in front of the Prophet (s). The Prophet (s) said to him, "Woe to you, you have cut off your companion's neck, you have cut off your companion's neck," repeating it several times and then added, "Whoever among you has to praise his brother should say, 'I think that he is so and so, and Allah knows exactly the truth, and I do not confirm anybody's good conduct before Allah, but I think him so and so,' if he really knows what he says about him." (Bukhari)

Often adults praise a child's work because they want the child's affection and they don't know what else to say. When presented with a child's work, the easiest response is to show some interest and maybe ask a question or two. "Oh, you made a tower with the blocks. Was it hard to get it that tall without knocking it down a few times?" "Tell me about your picture. Did the teacher suggest the subject or did you decide that yourself?" These kinds of discussions show our interest, which is a reward for the child right there. The child gets to talk about methods of work and how he or she made decisions. This is one of those good exercises that build a child's ability to express himself as mentioned in Chapter 3, Standing for Justice.

There is a place for big rewards. Every child dreams of something. Different families have different ideas of what "big" is. Big rewards should be spaced out so they are appreciated. They can be for special occasions, like finishing the memorization of a new surah, earning so many stars for doing chores on a monthly chores chart, or they can be just because we are a family and we enjoy some of life's pleasures from time to time. Alhamdulillah we have the health and the financial ability.

Thinking about rewards, we need to go back to the section on sadaqah in Chapter 3. All kinds of things can be sadaqah and receive reward from Allah. Children have school and play and there is time spent getting ready for things and taking care of life's basics, eating, sleeping, and cleaning up. By reclassifying some of these things, and adding a few more, our children can be spending much of their time doing good deeds, rewarded by both Allah and their parents.

Going to school and studying can be counted as good deeds as a child learns about the world Allah created and prepares himself to be an educated adult, ready to work in this world, to help his family and to help others. When eating, sleeping and taking care of the body Allah gave him, a child is working to stay healthy. It's a way of thanking Allah when we take care of the gifts He gave us. And we can use our bodies to help other people, which also pleases Allah, and increases our reward with Him.

All sorts of other small acts can count as good deeds for the child. As we know from the words of the Prophet (s), even a smile earns reward from Allah when it is done with the pure intention of pleasing Him. So what can a child do? She can take care of herself and her things so someone else doesn't have to. She can pitch in to help when someone else is doing a job. Can she help a parent fold laundry? How about sharing food with a friend or guest or comforting someone who got hurt? And, of course, a child can follow the rules and remind other children so the day goes more easily and maybe safer. There is no end to the list of kind, considerate, helpful things a child can do, even a young child.

At first a child will do these things to please herself and her parents. As she grows and learns more about Allah, she will be pleased to find that she is earning rewards from Allah by pleasing her parents. Gradually, she can advance to doing things on her own initiative just for the sake of pleasing Allah. Parents are the guides in this growing process.

Too much guidance can rob a child of a sense of initiative, restrict his desire to explore the world, and stifle his budding independence. We can't direct every minute of the day for our growing children. A middle-of-the-road, moderate, regular course is needed:

The Prophet (s) was asked, "What deeds are loved most by Allah?" He said, "The most regular constant deeds even though they may be few." He added, 'Don't take upon yourselves, except the deeds which are within your ability." (Bukhari)

Both children and adults need to reflect frequently on how we spend time and money and it may be helpful with older children to have family discussions of this hadith:

"The feet of the son of Adam shall not move from before his Lord on the Day of Judgement, until he is asked about five things: about his life and what he did with it, about his youth and what he wore it out in, about his wealth and how he earned it and spent it, and what he did with what he knew." (Tirmidhi).

A father can give his children examples of choices he made in deciding his career. Or he can tell them why he decided to buy a new car now rather than wait longer. In a family discussion to plan the family vacation, he can guide them in thinking about whether to visit grandparents again compared to an educational trip where they explore some historical sites. Which choice might get the best reward from Allah?

In teaching our children to act for the sake of pleasing Allah, we are teaching them to be useful, giving, caring people. Too many parents today fail to convey this message to their children and consequently end up with children who only know how to take and expect to be served - often by their parents.

Such attitudes do not suit Muslims, for Islam encourages self-sufficiency and discourages asking from others. It emphasizes serving and not being served, giving and not looking for favors, and doing one's end of things without expecting or waiting for others to do theirs. It is an active, not a passive life.

"By the One in Whose hand is my soul, if one of you were to take a rope and gather firewood on his back that would be better for him than coming to a man to whom Allah, the Mighty and Sublime, has given of His bounty and asking him (for help), which he may or may not give. (An-Nasa'i) [Gathering firewood was a way for the poor to earn money.]

"The upper hand is better than the lower hand (i.e. he who gives in charity is better than him who takes it). One should start giving first to his dependents. And the best object of charity is that which is given by a wealthy person (from the money which is left after his expenses). And whoever abstains from asking others for some financial help, Allah will give him and save him from asking others, Allah will make him self-sufficient." (Bukhari)

6 - STRATEGIES FOR DEALING WITH PROBLEMS

Know that your property and your children are no more than a source of testing for you and that with Allah lies your most substantial reward (Qur'an 8:28)

We will have problems with our children, no matter how perfectly we try to raise them and no matter how wonderful our children are. This chapter will describe five ways to address problems:

    a. Ignoring faults and errors
    b. Modifying the environment
    c. Allowing natural consequences
    d. Dealing with anger
    e. Seeking outside help

Some strategies only work with some problems. There is nothing golden about this list but insha Allah (if Allah wills) it will be a useful way for people to see their options and design solutions to their specific problems.

a. Ignoring Faults and Errors

This does not mean we ignore our children's faults and errors and leave them to do whatever they want. It does mean that when we start listing faults and errors, we can look at the list in perspective. We are not going to solve every problem. It would drive us and our children nuts if we tried to correct their every false move.

However, if you overlook (their faults), gloss over (their shortcomings) and forgive them, (know that) Allah is forgiving and merciful. (Qur'an 64:14-15)

In his prayers, Prophet Muhammad (s) asked Allah to forgive his faults. We turn to Allah to forgive our own faults and overlook them to hopefully focus on the good that we do. As we want Allah to forgive us, so we need to be forgiving with our children for some of the problems they have.

Jake came home an hour late from middle school. He had missed asr prayer and it's now maghrib and time for supper. He kicked off his muddy wet shoes and one flew into the kitchen, dirtying the floor. His mother noted his bad mood and just asked him quietly to clean up the mess of his shoe and wash for supper. She saw him go pray before he came back to the kitchen to eat. Later she asked him about his day. He'd stayed after school to work on a history assignment. It's due tomorrow but the other boy he's working with just fooled around at the library and they really hadn't gotten much done. He has a math test tomorrow he needs to study for, too.

Maybe Mom suspects it wasn't just the other boy fooling around at the library rather than working. Maybe Jake only realized the amount of work he had for the evening when he got home. But now is not the time for a lecture on homework or on missing prayers or kicking shoes off. Let him explain his history project and see how he can be encouraged to finish it off. Offer to help him with a few math problems from the unit he will be tested on. At least he remembered this time that he has a math test! Last month he was forgetting to turn in his math homework, getting zeros for it and never mentioned the test he had until he brought it home with a low mark. Maybe he can do a bit of math review in the morning if the history project takes too long.

There is a time to discuss how Jake keeps track of his homework and projects, but right now, he just needs emergency assistance. A lecture right now could be overwhelming and cause him to shut down. When he and his mom do discuss the problem, this evening can be used as an example of why he needs to change his system.

Children learn responsibility at different rates and for different things slowly over time. And the child who was very prompt at doing homework last year (or last month) may become very forgetful this year (or month), when their interest turns to other activities and social relationships. Hopefully by the time they are adults they will pull their act together and be organized and on time with their responsibilities.

Danah, age three, has been hitting her little brother when he bothers her, particularly when she is getting tired or hungry. Mom has to keep an eye on their play and is tired of intervening each time. Today Danah screamed at him and threw a toy onto the floor, but instead of slapping him, she turned away and stalked off in a huff. Danah's behavior may not be ideal but it is an improvement. Maybe she is learning not to hit? "Good job Danah. You may be upset, but you didn't hit." Remember that Allah promises us reward for the bad intentions we don't do.

In time Mom can work with Danah on not screaming and not throwing things but give Danah some time to solidly adopt the new habit of not hitting.

The one who covers the failings of someone in this world will have his shortcomings covered by Allah on the Day of Judgment. (Muslim)

Ignoring faults and errors is particularly important when there are outside influences on the child. If a child is going back and forth between homes following a divorce, each parent needs to be aware of rules that are different at the other house. It is hard for children to follow two sets of rules. Then at school there is another set of rules. And the before and after-school care center may have different rules. This doesn't mean parents can't have their own rules. But they will need to be thoughtful and maybe a bit indulgent in enforcing them so they don't stress their children too much, particularly in the beginning stages of lifestyle change for their children.

b. Modifying the Environment

This strategy is similar to the ideas under Controlling the Environment in Chapter 4, but it is undertaken as a plan for dealing with problems that can come up when children's ability to control themselves is limited. So it is usually used with younger children although it can be very useful in some situations with older children.

All children manage life better when they've had enough sleep and they aren't hungry. Being sick can also cause children to be tired and irritable. Parents can plan ahead and set up schedules so their child's basic needs are met. They observe their child in different situations and learn special details about how the child copes with missing a meal or having a meal delayed, staying up late at night, or missing naptime. Then they adapt plans to avoid stressing their child out. One child may be fine if meals are delayed. He just seems to rest and go quiet for a short bit and then gets back into playing nicely. Another child becomes cranky and gets into fights with siblings almost every day about a half hour before family mealtime. While the first child doesn't have a problem, the second child probably needs a light snack, an apple or a small serving of yogurt or something, an hour or so before mealtime if mealtime can't be changed.

Another form of modifying the environment is to set up the home so parents don't have to be continually yelling "watch out" or "don't touch that." Children are born explorers and have a lot of energy. They are also very good at finding shortcuts to getting what they want with the least effort, like grabbing their brother's scissors from the table rather than looking in their book bag for their own.

There are some toddlers who explore Mom's houseplants once or twice, get redirected each time, and then ignore them. So the houseplants can stay where Mom organized them before she had children. Other toddlers seem fascinated by plants and love to pull at the leaves, put the leaves in their mouths, and end up knocking everything over if they aren't restrained. Their mothers need to move the houseplants out of reach or get rid of them.

This may solve some problems for older children too. Rosa has just started high school and her first report card isn't good. She isn't getting her homework done or studying well. Last year she seemed to be slipping into bad habits but she had still done all right. When she was younger she was a very good student with good grades. Mom sat down to talk with her. The library is only a fifteen minute safe walk from home. How about going there to study after school and Mom or Dad can pick her up before supper, or when she phones them she's done. Rosa is surprised and unsure about this idea. But Mom talks about her being older and capable of being responsible for her studies on her own. Besides, if she needs help, she can ask the reference librarian right there.

They agree to try out this setup for studying. The first day Rosa noticed the exercise of walking to the library seemed to clear her head. It was relaxing and a bit liberating to be out on a mission of her own. At the library she found a table to set herself up. Surrounded by quiet adults reading she felt mature and serious. She settled into her homework. Over time her grades improved. She got help often from the reference librarian for her history projects, which made them a lot easier to do, and the librarian even knew how to find video demonstrations for some math and science problems occasionally. Her mother or father sometimes stopped in early to pick her up and to casually check that she was really working. They were proud of how well she was doing, and told her so.

This won't work with every child. Maybe someone else would waste the time playing games on the library computers rather than studying. It won't take long to find out if parents insist on seeing test results and do spot checks on homework. And it's good to test our children occasionally to see how mature they can be.

For Allah wishes ease and not hardship. (Qur'an 2:185)

Muntaha and Hassan have a home office in their house and two children who like to do art projects and school work, but the children don't always bring their markers and scissors home from school. They lose their things too. And going to their bedrooms upstairs to get their equipment from supplies there is harder than raiding the office for pencils and glue and paper. Raiding the office is an appropriate term because they often move things around and papers get messed up. Also, Hassan doesn't realize until a week later that they have taken all his permanent markers and he needs them, but the children are off playing at the neighbors.

The couple have tried telling the children not to touch the desk or storage closet in the office, but since the raids aren't everyday occurrences, the children tend to forget. They say they are just borrowing something for a minute, but they forget to put it back, or they put it back somewhere it doesn't belong. To modify the environment Hassan starts using the locks of the desk drawers and installs one on the storage closet. Then he and Muntaha agree to keep all papers off the desktop so they can't be messed up.

Time-Out

Sometimes situations come up that we haven't planned for and we need to change the environment on the spot. This is a place for a time-out. Time-outs are described variously in childcare books, but what we want to describe here is a method for removing a child or children from a social situation where they have lost control of themselves and are getting too excited and careless or too angry, or just too emotional to behave reasonably. It is also used when they exercise poor judgement, like saying bad words to someone else or they are otherwise being mean.

This is not a punishment and shouldn't be ordered by an angry parent. We shouldn't wait till we are angry to impose a time-out. We need to be proactive.

The children are engaged in a hide and seek game that is getting out of hand with children running and screaming and shouts of "You cheated!" If Dad calls out "Time-out!" older children may settle down by themselves. Younger ones will need Dad to referee who to put on the sidelines for a few minutes rest.

When the children are bickering in the back seat of the car and Mom has a headache from the noise, she can pull over to the side of the road and announce a time-out. She can wait there quietly until the kids realize and ask her what's wrong. She can tell them she needs some quiet time to drive and they can continue on their way when they give her that quiet. When they settle down, she can start driving again.

The four-year-old twins have been playing nicely for a while but they are getting tired. Saleem built a fort with blocks and Salman has been playing with the cars. Suddenly Salman rams his big truck into Saleem's fort, knocking it down. "Wow, look at that!" he cries. Saleem's cry is in rage. "No!" "Mommy, Salman hit my fort!"

Mom tells Salman, "Two minute time-out Salman. That's not acceptable behavior. We don't crash other people's things."

Salman argues back, "He finished building it. He didn't need it. I did a cool crash!"

Mom responds, "Salman, three minute time-out, starting now." And she points to the clock. Salman walks over to the sofa upset and sits down. He knows the routine. Mom helps Saleem collect his blocks and gets him busy setting them up again. This way he is getting the attention, not his brother.

Three minutes later (approximately) Salman is back from the sofa. He picks up his truck and asks Saleem, "Can I see how it crashes down?"

"No. I'm still building. Maybe later," answers his brother.

If a parent finds that they are ordering time-outs over and over again, they probably need to think about modifying the environment further. Maybe one child is too immature to play nicely with the group and needs a smaller group or a different schedule so she gets more naptime? Maybe the chemistry between Hisham and Kelly is just too volatile and they each need different playmates? Maybe playtimes are too long and children need a snack or lunch to refuel? With our complex lives, we tend to fall into habits but sometimes we need to make efforts to reorganize so we aren't putting our children into situations where they get too stressed and can't behave well.

As children get older, a parent can ask them if they need a time-out. That may be enough to get them to take control of themselves. Parents can gradually train the child to time herself rather than them setting a specific time limit. This demonstrates that the action is not punitive but a basic method of working on self-control.

We all need a method for moving away from situations where we might lose control, particularly people with quick tempers. Parents can model the technique. When a salesclerk is being very rude and unreasonable, Amina can take herself and her children out of the way for a few minutes to calm herself down, and then return to address the problem in a calmer manner.

For older children and for parents, salah can be a time-out. When we are upset or out of sorts, leaving to wash for salah and doing some extra salah and/or du'a can bring us peace. Sometimes Allah suggests solutions to our problems during these times of peace too.

Substitution

This is another form of modifying the environment. We divert children from what we don't want them to do by telling them to do something else or offering them something else. So, if toddler Ahmed is playing with his sister's backpack, distract him with a ball or another thing, without mentioning that he shouldn't mess with her backpack. If we don't like a TV show our children are watching, we can just tell them they've been spending too much time inside, turn the TV off, and send them out, without mentioning that the TV show is inappropriate and complaining that they should have turned it off themselves.

There is no need to be repeating rules over and over again and emphasizing the bad aspect of actions all the time. This is sometimes called "distract and redirect." Actually this method is particularly important with older children who already know the rules and hate to hear lectures about them. It is often said, affection is more important than perfection. Let's create a warm positive relationship with our children. Teens, especially, are more likely to remember and follow rules if they have a good relationship with us.

Hakeem has just started high school and is hanging out with a new group of friends. His older cousin mentions to Hakeem's mom that one of the boys in Hakeem's group is known to sell illegal drugs at school. So when Hakeem asks if he can join the chess club, she agrees, even though it means someone has to pick him up from school twice a week. His father suggests that Hakeem start going to judo classes again. They had stopped the classes a few years ago because of the expense, but now it sounds like a good investment to Hakeem's parents. Gradually Hakeem is so involved in school work, chess, and judo that he isn't hanging out with that group anymore. And his parents never had to say a word about their fears.

The Prophet (s) himself, after hearing people explain themselves, often asked people, "May I tell you about something that is better than this?" before offering them advice.

135

It is a part of the excellence of a believer's faith that he leaves off whatever is of no benefit to him in this world and the Hereafter. (Tirmidhi)

Jealousy

A special issue that requires modifying the environment is dealing with jealousy among children. Jealousy is a common emotion among siblings. We remember the stories of Cain and Abel, and Joseph and his brothers.

The example above of the twins, Saleem and Salman, might have been caused by jealousy. Maybe Mom made a passing comment, "Cool fort, Saleem." Salman was playing with cars and trucks and has nothing for her to comment on. Ten minutes later he crashes his truck into the fort. A feeling of envy can come over a child quickly. That doesn't mean Mom needs to treat the situation differently. It might not have been jealousy, but a moment of resentment. Allah knows the truth. If Mom reflects later, she can consider if she might accidently be playing favorites or if there are really signs of jealousy. When parents think ahead about controlling the environment, and giving a place and attention to each child, jealousy may never develop. But even the best of efforts might not work all the time.

Special circumstances may increase the likelihood of problems with jealousy: the arrival of a new baby, the arrival of step-children or foster children into the family, a disability or exceptional ability that makes one child need more attention or draw on more of the family resources, or a divorce where children feel drawn to support one parent over another. When these circumstances occur, parents should check for issues. While the family is adjusting to the changes brought on by these circumstances, parents need to make an extra effort to see that each child feels valued by both parents.

To prepare Aliyah for the approaching birth of a new sister, her mother started changing the environment by encouraging Aliyah to do things for herself and praising her independence. Aliyah got a new "big girl" bed and her old crib was stored away for a few months. Although Mama didn't like the mess, she let Aliyah feed herself more and encouraged her. She let Aliyah attempt more activities on the park playground and found ways to mention off and on how she loved having a big girl who could do things for herself. She started asking Aliyah to fetch small things for her or to turn on the light or do other little things to "help" her mother, each time with a little comment of praise about being a big girl. Then when the baby came, Aliyah's parents got her a "big sister" shirt and made her feel special. She got to hold the baby when she was sitting safely on the sofa next to Daddy. She got to run and get the burp cloth for Mama. She got to turn on the lullaby music in the baby's room when they put the baby to bed. Daddy took more time with Alia so she wouldn't notice all the time Mama spent with the baby. With all the preemptive planning and actions, Aliyah didn't show signs of being jealous of her new sister.

In circumstances of stepchildren living together, it is probably best to ask the children to call their father's new wife "Aunt" and their mother's new husband "Uncle." This helps keep it out in the open that the relationships are different. My father's wife is not my mom. I can have many aunts and different relationships with each. I may have a better relationship with my aunt than I do with my mother, but my aunt isn't in competition with my mom.

When a woman asks her children to call her new husband "Daddy," she is, in effect, trying to replace their father in the children's lives. Maybe she is just thinking of their daily lives with friends and school, so the children don't have to explain the situation to everyone. Maybe the children's father is really out of the picture. But the biological father has rights that Allah gave him, and we shouldn't interfere with that.

Calling a step-father man "Uncle" while his children call him "Dad" clarifies situations that could create jealousy. It becomes more natural for him to favor his own children over his stepchildren, recognizing a tendency that is probably there anyway. How we set up the environment for the children can make a big difference in how children identify themselves and feel at home. Like any uncle, when a man treats the kids to ice cream, he treats all the kids equally. But with other items, like school supplies and clothes, he might pay for his stepchildren only if their parents can't.

With older children we can discuss issues of envy and jealousy. We teach children to say "Alhamdulillah" (thanks be to Allah) when they receive something and "Masha'Allah" (Allah willed it) when someone else has something good happen to them. We will have what Allah has set up for

137

us and others will have different things. We trust in Allah that we will never be the losers in life when we accept what He has provided.

Pointing out the terrible evils of envy, the Prophet (s) said:

"No one of you becomes a true believer until he likes for his brother what he likes for himself". (Riyad as-Salihin, Bukhari, Muslim)

Do not hate each other; do not envy each other; do not desert each other; and be the servants of Allah in brotherhood. It is not allowed for a Muslim to keep apart from his brother for more than three days. (Abu Dawud)

c. Allowing Natural Consequences

Allah sends tests our way and we struggle with them. We live through the consequences of our decisions. Our children need to learn how to do that too. We want our children to grow up to be strong, independent, and capable to manage the difficulties of life. They need to be challenged and they need to take some risks. We have to provide some safety net, to make sure they don't overextend themselves and their developmental ability, but we need to do it in a thoughtful moderate way.

All you people! Be mindful of your Lord, and fear the day when no parent will be able to do anything for his own child, nor any child for his parent. (Qur'an 31:33)

Children start learning early. A toddler tries to get a vase of flowers on the shelf and pulls the vase down on top of himself, splashing himself with water and knocking his knee and foot with the vase. He is learning which objects are easy to reach for and pull down and which ones require more care to move.

We should probably put vases of flowers up where our toddlers can't pull them down, but they can learn the same lesson from pulling less breakable things down from shelves, things that won't hurt them too much. But creating a safe play environment doesn't mean keeping children in a room of soft pillows. They learn from climbing the jungle gym at the park, and from climbing trees too. We give them safety helmets, but we let them ride bikes. They can get wet trying to cross the creek and get blisters from raking leaves. These are all healthy activities for children to learn how to move their bodies and how to take care of them.

Some consequences occur because children make bad choices. Allowing these to take their natural course will, hopefully, teach children to make better choices.

A young girl screams in rage because she wanted the other cookie from the plate, and throws the one she got on the floor, breaking it into pieces. If her father refuses to give her another, she learns to accept the first cookie she puts her hand on and that tantrums aren't useful behavior.

If we feel sorry for our children and try to make everything right for them quickly, they won't learn some very important lessons.

John has an essay due tomorrow morning and a math test. He's known about the assignments for a few days. Two days ago his friend invited him to go ice skating tonight. He asks his father if he can go skating and do his homework later in the evening. But John will be very tired by then and he isn't doing that well in math. Yesterday he told his parents he had no homework and he spent the evening playing games. So Dad tells him "No". School work and rest are more important than extra activities. John has heard his parents' advice about not leaving homework till the last minute and his father had reminded him of the proposed skating event yesterday when John said he had no homework.

Hiba, age twelve, forgot to take her lunch to school and has no money to buy lunch. Her mother has brought her lunch to her before when she forgot it, several times and Hiba knows it's hard for her mom to get it over to Hiba's school and still get to her job on time. They have discussed how she prepares for school in the morning and made plans for ensuring all her books, homework, school supplies, and lunch get into her backpack. There is a check list for her on the wall near where she stores her backpack. If her mother drives over to the school again to take it to her, Hiba has no reason to become more responsible. But if she goes without lunch for the day, she may remember her lunch the following day.

Our religion also teaches us that it is our responsibility to follow up on our errors with good deeds. As much as they are capable, children should clean up their spills and fix what they break. If they can't do that, they might do something else for the person they harm to make up for their error.

It's raining and Arsalan has been drawing and coloring at the kitchen table for a while now. He is bored and feeling restless. His father has been on the phone at his desk for a while now and he's not supposed to bother Daddy when he's on the phone working. Markers are strewn around on the table and it occurs to Arsalan that the red would look cool on the yellow kitchen wall. Then he tries the black and the green. The green doesn't show up as well as the other colors so the tree he draws with it doesn't look that good. At age four, Arsalan knows you don't draw on walls, but he isn't thinking of that right now. Then he hears his father walk into the room.

"Hey, Arsalan, how's it going?" his father asks. There's no need for Arsalan to reply. His face is subdued and he looks unhappy. Daddy's voice reminded him that he shouldn't be drawing on the wall. Daddy will see what he did. Daddy looks around the room. He sees the drawing on the wall and feels anger and frustration. Arsalan should know better by now not to draw on the walls. Then he remembers that Arsalan was coloring for a fair amount of time. That phone call he was on did take more time than he expected. He should have checked up on the boy a while ago.

"Get a cleaning rag and put a little water on it and wash the wall, Arsalan," he says. Arsalan goes to the drawer of cleaning rags and pulls one out. Daddy needs to help him wet it and wring it out so water won't drip all over. Then Arsalan wipes the wall down. Most of the marker disappears but the black is resistant. Arsalan rubs harder. Daddy notices too and he looks over at the markers on the table. The black permanent marker they use to label items they store in the freezer is among the markers on the table.

"That black isn't going to come off with water, Arsalan. I'll have to use something stronger on it later," Daddy tells him. Daddy picks up the permanent marker and shows it to Arsalan. "This isn't your marker. See how it doesn't clean up? It's permanent and we only use it on labels for the freezer so the labels will stay. It's hard to remove. Please don't use it again if you see it out." Then Daddy put the permanent marker back in its storage place on a high shelf. Either he or his wife must have forgotten to put it away last time it was used.

Yasir, age ten, broke his older brother's remote-controlled car, allowing it to crash off the bridge outside and fall into the creek. The car is ruined beyond repair. He had begged for days to be allowed to play with it but his brother kept saying he wouldn't be careful. Finally his brother had given him permission.

Yasir doesn't have the money to buy his brother a new one. Is there something else he can do to help his brother? Maybe he can take over some chore of his brother's, like taking out the garbage for a week (a month)? Let the two boys discuss it and see what they might agree to. Maybe his brother will only ask that he not touch his brother's things ever again or will forgive him and not ask for anything. Maybe one of their parents will need to help them along with their discussion. It is a learning experience for both boys to try to work something out.

For good deeds remove evil deeds. (Qur'an 11:114)

Allah's Messenger (s) said, "Whoever has wronged his brother, should ask for his pardon (before his death), as (in the Hereafter) there will be neither a dinar nor a dirham [dinar and dirham are names of money]. *(He should secure pardon in this life) before some of his good deeds are taken and paid to his brother, or, if he has done no good deeds, some of the bad deeds of his brother are taken to be loaded on him (in the Hereafter)." (Bukhari)*

Lying is one of the major sins in Islam. It is also probably one of the most commonly committed of those sins among adults, so it is important that we teach our children to avoid lying. Of course as was discussed in "Standing for Justice" in Chapter 3, children develop their ability to understand the difference between truth and fiction over time. They learn how to describe things accurately as they grow. We need to encourage them to be accurate. When they do get old enough to know what lying is and do it deliberately, we need to draw their attention to it and make sure they realize how important it is not to lie. Parents should impress on children the seriousness of lying, but they also should be aware of the developmental stages that may affect children. They may not tell the truth because of immaturity, impulsiveness, a desire to protect or impress someone, or a fear of consequences, even after they have learned what lying is. They still need time to grow and develop. We need to be careful how we address their behavior, holding them accountable where appropriate and giving them some breathing room where appropriate.

All children probably try lying from time to time. When parents don't take the time to check up on what their children say, lying can become a habit.

"Did you make your bed and put your lunch in your book bag?" Mom asks her daughter, Dalia, as they hurry to get her off to school. "Yes Mom." Later, when they return home in the evening, Mom notices that the bed wasn't made and she finds Dalia's lunch still in the refrigerator. But by then Mom can't remember if she said anything about it in the morning, so Dalia's lie goes uncaught. "Didn't I ask you if you had your lunch with you this morning?" "What? Oh, it was ok. I got a lunch at school." Dalia avoids answering her mother about whether her mother asked her about her lunch in the morning or explaining why she said yes when she really didn't take it.

Raising children takes time. We need to check up on what is going on and teach them the important things in life. Making a bed isn't that important. Dalia likes to "forget" her homemade lunch on Wednesdays because the school serves pizza that day, and kids who forget their lunch get served because the school always has some extras. If Mom knew, there would be nothing wrong with sending lunch money for Wednesday as long as the pizza is halal. She should talk about all this with Dalia so Dalia can see that what she was hiding wasn't worth lying about.

A woman asked the Prophet (s), "If one of us women said that she had no desire for a certain thing even though she had that desire, would it be considered a lie?" The prophet (s) said, "Falsehood is written as falsehood, and a small falsehood is written as a small falsehood." (Muslim)

142

In our busy world we can't check up on our children all the time. And it is good to create an environment of trust. But from time to time we need to make the effort to check up on what we are being told. When there is a supportive, loving environment between parents and children, children are more likely to talk to their parents, more likely to admit that they lied, and less likely to lie. Then, if we find out our child has lied, we need to make time for a serious talk and some consequences. The best consequence should be a change in the environment to "lack of trust". The child already knows what a trusting environment is like. Now he or she can experience the opposite.

Mom has already talked to Dalia about lying before and she knows they've had lessons on it at the mosque, so Dalia knows clearly she shouldn't lie. But lying is common in society today. Children may hear it all over.

If Mom caught Dalia lying in the example here, then the next morning she would ask Dalia, "Did you make your bed and put your lunch in your book bag?" If Dalia says yes, she could then say, "Do I need to check myself or are you being truthful today?" And then she should do a quick check and insist anything not done be done, even if it makes Dalia late for school. Part of Dalia's reason for lying is to give herself fewer chores to do in the morning.

Mom should carry this checking over into other things. "Homework done?" If Dalia says yes, Mom should insist on checking that her "yes" is true. Dalia says she is studying at the library. Mom should show up and check up on her. She gets permission to go to a friend's home. Mom should phone the friend's mom and ask to speak with Dalia to tactfully check that she is there.

Hopefully she won't find Dalia is doing anything wrong behind her back. Then slowly she can work with Dalia toward going back to a relationship of trust. Distrust creates a strained relationship. Trust creates comfort. Normally a child will want to go to the more comfortable relationship and will learn the value of a relationship of trust.

Parents need to be careful that they aren't setting a bad example for their children, like the classic example of the parent telling the child to lie to a person on the phone and say the parent isn't home when really the parent just doesn't want to talk to that person. For another example of parents lying, some people feel that promising things to children to get them to behave is fine, even if they have no intention of giving them anything. "Let's get ready for bed quickly so we have time for a story" (and then Mom gets the kids in bed and leaves them with no story). This is deliberate lying.

If someone calls a child, saying that he will give him a certain thing, and he doesn't give it, it is a lie. (Ahmad, similar in Abu Dawud)

Even if the lie was to cover something big, like to hide some embarrassing thing we have done, it isn't worth the sin. The best talk is to say what is good or keep silent. Actually, it is quite good to cover our faults or errors, conceal our sins, and to be embarrassed about them. It shows our consciences are working when we are embarrassed by things we have done. We can teach this to children by not talking about their errors except with the essential people who are needed to help.

Selma called her teacher a bad name at school yesterday and the teacher called home to complain. Khalil got caught playing with matches and trying to smoke a cigarette. Both parents probably need to know what happened and how the situation was handled, but the neighbors and the children's friends don't need to hear the stories. Selma's mom doesn't need to tell people that Selma is working on anger management problems. Khalil's parents don't need to tell anyone that he tried smoking.

In asking someone for help with a situation, it is often better to ask indirectly, unless we are dealing with a professional who will keep the conversation confidential. Khalil's mom could ask her friend, a social worker she trusts who can keep things confidential, "I heard kids my son's age sometimes try smoking. Khalil's father smokes and he has regular visits at his dad's house. How can I teach Khalil not to smoke? Do you know any advice or where I can go for advice?"

Allah doesn't like for bad news to be announced in public, except where injustice has been done (Qur'an 4:148)

Whoever believes in Allah and the Last Day should talk what is good or keep quiet, and whoever believes in Allah and the Last Day should not hurt (or insult) his neighbor… (Bukhari)

There is an issue in teaching children to be tactful that needs to be remembered when we are teaching them about lying. There are polite ways of responding to a person without lying that avoid saying a truth that would hurt the person.

Mahmut, age 10, is a fussy eater at home. His family has been invited to eat dinner at a neighbor's house, and his mother knows the neighbor is making spaghetti, because the neighbor told her. Mahmut doesn't like spaghetti at all but his mother heard there would be other food on the menu too. Before they left for the dinner, Mahmut's mother can ask him to sit and talk with her. She can explain that she expects spaghetti to be on the menu but there will be other things too and she hopes he will find something he likes to eat. They don't know this neighbor very well and she might be hurt if he tells her that he doesn't like spaghetti. But Mom needs to be clear she is not asking him to lie. Not saying he doesn't like it isn't a lie. If the neighbor asks him to put some spaghetti on his plate, he can just say he'd rather have something else now. If she asks him if he likes spaghetti, it is not a lie to say he prefers another food.

This kind of response to people is tactful. It is part of the manners of Islam to speak in a thoughtful polite way.

There are only three types of lies that are allowed in Islam.

I do not count as a liar a man who puts things right between people, saying a word by which he intends only putting things right, and a man who says something in war, and a man who says something to his wife, or a wife who says something to her husband. (Abu Dawud)

This is understood to mean that a man can tell his wife she is the most beautiful woman in the world and Allah will not worry this this is not the most complete truth. And a woman can tell her husband that his receding hairline makes him look older and more distinguished.

One woman had a coworker she doesn't care for. "The only thing she ever did right was make that pie they served at the picnic," she told her friend, another coworker. Then to make peace, her friend could tell the other woman, "What do you mean, you think she hates you? Just yesterday she was telling me how much she appreciated the pie you made for the picnic." We should use these exceptions very carefully to avoid making errors.

I asked the Messenger of Allah (s), "How can salvation be achieved?" He replied, "Control your tongue, keep to your house, and weep over your sins." (Riyad as-Salihin, Tirmidhi)

d. Dealing with Anger

One of the biggest problems for everyone is controlling our anger. People do all kinds of negative things when they get angry, like yelling, using bad language, hurting other people or things. Anger can be an important emotion and can motivate a person to stand up to injustice and oppression. Someone who never gets angry enough to set limits is at risk of being abused. We need to feel anger in order to stand up for what we believe is right. What we are concerned about is keeping anger under control so we don't do things or say things that are bad.

Allah (swt) praises people who control their anger:

Race together towards your Lord's forgiveness and to a garden as wide as the heavens and the earth – reserved only for those who were mindful (of Allah). They spent (in the cause of Allah) in good times and bad, restrained their temper and overlooked the faults of others. (Qur'an 3:133-34)

And Prophet Muhammad (s) frequently gave people advice about anger:

A man said to the Prophet (s), "Give me (some) advice." He said, "Do not be angry." He (the man) repeated his question several times. The Prophet said, "Do not be angry." (Riyad as-Salihin, Bukhari, Tirmidhi)

The strong one is not the one who throws (people) down, but the strong one is the one who controls himself in the face of anger. (Bukhari, Muslim)

Children often feel strong emotions and they can switch between emotions quickly. Hadi, age 2, is mad at his brother, age 3, so he shoves him, and his brother falls down. Hadi immediately starts to cry because he sees his brother is hurt so both boys are crying. Two minutes later the boys are laughing as they run after the ball Hadi accidently kicked while he was crying. At this stage of life we don't need to worry too much about the anger.

As they grow older and their emotional states last longer, we need to start teaching them how to control it. Time-outs are a good way for this. It's not a punishment but a way to give a child time for the emotional uproar to calm down. In many cases with children, just calming down is enough because there isn't really an issue to deal with.

Hafsa, age 5, got to the dinner table late and Tasnim, age 4, got the blue cup first. Hafsa got angry and kicked the chair. Mom had her sit quietly for two minutes to calm down. Then she joined the family for dinner. Mom can then ask the girls to explain why the blue cup caused a problem and hopefully help them resolve that problem.

Prophet Muhammad (s) mentioned doing something like this:

"When one of you becomes angry while standing, he should sit down. If the anger leaves him, well and good; otherwise he should lie down." (Abu Dawud).

Another thing she could have done is ask Hafsa to go wash again to calm down.

Anger comes from the devil, the devil was created of fire, and fire is extinguished only with water; so when one of you becomes angry, he should perform wudu. (Abu Dawud)

If there is some issue to deal with, it can be better handled once everyone is calm. We all think better that way. And we should deal with the issues.

147

Ignoring those issues means we will have continual problems with them and anger levels will likely increase.

With older children we can give the advice from Qur'an as well, although the cooling off methods will remain important:

And if an evil suggestion from Satan incites you, seek refuge in Allah. Truly, He is All-Hearing, All-Knowing. (Qur'an 7:200)

While I was sitting in the company of the Prophet, two men abused each other and the face of one of them became red with anger, and his jugular veins swelled (i.e. he became furious). On that the Prophet said, "I know a word, the saying of which will cause him to relax, if he does say it. If he says: 'I seek Refuge with Allah from Satan.' then all his anger will go away." Somebody said to him, "The Prophet has said, 'Seek refuge with Allah from Satan.'" The angry man said, "Am I crazy?" [The angry man denied that he was angry.] *(Bukhari, Muslim)*

Parents should to do a check of their own anger and how they manage it. Sometimes we need the time-out. And we ought to check that we aren't giving a child a time-out when we are stressed out and they haven't done anything. We need to be role models for our children so—if we are modeling anger and negative behavior—that is not just bad for us but it is also teaching things to them we don't want them to do.

"Do not invoke a curse on yourselves, and do not invoke a curse on your children, and do not invoke a curse on your servants, and do not invoke a curse on your property, lest you happen to do it at a time when Allah is asked for something and grants your request." (Abu Dawud)

Al-Ghazali, the twelfth century Islamic scholar, wrote extensively about anger in his book, *Revival of Religious Learning*. He described three things that protect a person from out-of-control anger; focusing the mind on more necessary things, focusing on the oneness of Allah, and, (with the knowledge that Allah doesn't like anger), loving Allah more than the things of the world.

He also offered a list of useful thoughts to consider when we are working to control our anger:

- Remember the reward promised in Qur'an from Allah for not being angry.
- Warn yourself of Allah's punishment in the Hereafter for acting on your anger.
- Fear the retaliation your enemy may take on you.
- Remember how ugly an angry person looks and how a person who restrains anger looks like a sober, educated person.
- Remember that the Devil will tell you that you will look weak if you don't express anger. Don't listen to him.
- Accept Allah's Will when circumstances are beyond your control.

We learn to control our emotions in stages. A child with an angry face may yell, "Sorry!" at her friend. She has learned the right words to say and that this is the time to say them, but she hasn't mastered the physical control of her face and her breathing. It's a step in the right direction and we should not scold the child. Maybe she will advance to the mastery stage on her own, the next time she gets angry. If she seems stuck at this stage, her parent might coach her to repeat her apology again. "Ok Lily, take a deep breath and try that a second time. "Sorry, Terry. I shouldn't have snatched the ball."

Older children and adults may try to use du'a (informal prayer). "Allah forgive me" or "I seek refuge with Allah from Satan" are common ones. Repeating these du'a under their breath as they calm down can sound like muttering something bad to those who can't hear them properly, or if the du'a are said in Arabic and the listener doesn't know the Arabic, particularly because they may look and sound angry. We need to be aware of this possibility. Using du'a like this is a good sign of advancing in self-control. Over time, these efforts lead to much greater anger control.

Once we and our children are in control we need to use our intelligence to figure out a good solution to any problems we may have.

On the school bus Orhan, a high school sophomore, usually sits by himself. His family just moved here six months ago and he hasn't found friends in his neighborhood where his family is the only Muslim family and the only family with dark skin. He's heard a few kids call him "that Taliban guy" a few times. There wasn't an opportunity for him to tell them he's part Turkish and part African-American. The African-Americans have been among the few to be friendly to him at school.

Today the boys in the seats on the other side of the bus aisle are talking happily about the football game they will play Saturday, boasting about their abilities on the field. Then they start jeering at Orhan, how they could beat the Taliban too, on the battlefield. One of the boys starts to use bad language to describe Orhan's mother. Orhan's anger boils but he grits his teeth and silently recites du'a, trying to focus on the words he is saying and ignore the words he is hearing in his ears from those around him. Finally the bus arrives at his stop and he can get off the bus.

Too upset to just go home and do his homework, Orhan wanders around the neighborhood for a while, imagining what he could have said to stop those kids. Each scenario is more unlikely than the last and he knows it. He feels powerless, alone. If he reports the boys, they will deny what they said. He doesn't think any of the other kids who heard them will support him against them and he isn't even sure who the other kids are.

The other boys are engaged in slander and insult, so they are giving Orhan from their good deeds or taking bad deeds from his account when he is patient and avoiding doing something bad himself. So with Allah, he is not losing when he ignores them. The Prophet (s) himself endured bad treatment like this. When he is calm again he can start thinking of ways to stay away from them. Maybe he can try sitting close to the driver, up front. The kids would be less likely to bother him there and, if they do, he would have a witness.

If he can ignore those kids and just do his best in school, maybe Allah will give him a chance to impress others and increase the number of friends he has there. Maybe even one of the bullies from the bus may become his friend. It takes time to develop friendships but he will be doing projects with others in his class and get to know them better. He can join some of the clubs or sport teams according to his interests and abilities. Usually there are a few vocal kids who set a tone harassing someone, but there are other quieter, thoughtful kids who are willing to be friends. The task for Orhan is to avoid assuming the vocal kids represent the majority opinion of the kids at his school. He needs to keep himself open to the possibility that many of the other kids don't all share in those negative stereotypes.

If Orhan could talk to his parents about the problem they might be able to help him. But older children often don't confide in their parents, especially if they lack an open relationship with their parents. If we can be supportive, non-judgmental, and ask open-ended questions, this can engage our older children to feel safe enough to share their concerns with us. We need to support them in joining clubs or activities that will give them a good social life as well as keep them reasonably occupied. In any case we need to encourage them to invite their friends over to our houses and drive them, if necessary, to visit their friends. If we have met their friends and the parents of their friends, we can be more connected with our children's lives.

With younger children, parents can go talk with the teacher when they learn of bullying. With older children it's harder because there often isn't one teacher who really knows what is going on. If it is a problem in one class then the first step is to talk to the teacher. If that doesn't help resolve the problem, the next step up is to report the problem to the principal. If that doesn't seem to be working, parents can bring the problem to the schoolboard. Most schools today have policies to address bullying and harassment. The often have assigned people on staff, and sometimes among students as well, who are tasked with addressing bullying and harassment complaints. Sometimes it takes an outside civil rights organization to send in a professional negotiator to work on improving a school's environment for minority children. Bullying is definitely a hardship. We need to work to overcome it and hopefully make our schools safer places for our children.

Goodness and evil are not equal, so ward off (evil) by doing good. That's how you can turn your enemy into your close supporter and ally. (Qur'an 41:34)

e. Seeking Outside Help

The list of parenting issues people have today is very long and complex. There are issues with the personalities of the child and/or parents that clash. There are issues with intellectual disabilities and mental illnesses. There are issues with interference from other people or overcoming trauma, like homelessness, divorce, major illness, and others. For all of these concerns there is help.

The first help is through patience and prayer, seeking guidance from Allah. We have the promise in Qur'an (2:286, 65:2-3) from Allah that He will never give us something harder than we can bear. When we turn to Him and ask for His help, He is shy to turn us away empty-handed. (Tirmidhi) This gives us strength in confronting our problems and prevents us from falling into despair and depression. We will either overcome the problem or Allah will generously reward us for our efforts, though often in ways we don't expect. And He is the source of all healing.

When I am sick, He cures me. (Qur'an 26:80)

And the second help is from human sources. Traditionally people called on their extended family for support, and this may still be a very good help where it exists. Today many families network through their social friends to find support. These informal networks may not be up on the latest research on parenting and child development, so we need to be careful of the advice we receive from them, but they know us and our children and they really care about us. Mom finds her child has a bedwetting problem. Then an aunt confides that two other children in the family have had this problem. Mom will still need medical advice, but knowing it is genetic can be helpful. There may be several members of the family with anxiety issues so there is a reservoir of understanding of the problem. When others in the family learn another child has the problem, they may be more tactful with that child and help Mom implement any strategies the child's doctor has prescribed. And when parents are having a fight with each other or with their child, family members and wise community members have a strong interest in helping resolve the dispute.

If two factions among the faithful get into a disagreement, then you must make peace between them. If one of them goes beyond (what's fair) against the other (group), then you must fight against the one that's going out of bounds until they comply with the command of Allah. If they do comply, then make peace between them with justice, and be sure to be evenhanded, for Allah loves those who are evenhanded. (Qur'an 49:9-10)

"The deeds of people would be presented every week on two days, Monday and Thursday, and every believing servant would be granted pardon except the one in whose (heart) there is bitterness against his brother and it would be said, Leave them and put them off until they are turned to reconciliation. " (Muslim)

"He who makes peace between the people by inventing good information or saying good things, is not a liar." (Bukhari)

Aysha is very concerned about her daughter Daisy. Daisy is seven but she still won't sit quietly to do homework. It takes an hour sometimes to get her to complete one worksheet for one class. Anything seems to distract her. She wiggles around in her chair, gets up and walks around the room, and she can talk nonstop. Aysha tried being firm, removed distractions from the room, and offered rewards, but Daisy can't seem to settle. The teacher said all the homework shouldn't take longer than a half hour a night and a friend confirmed her daughter finishes the work in fifteen to twenty minutes. Grandpa tried to help but he got frustrated and gave up quickly.

In the past, people would have labeled children like Daisy as lazy or dumb. Some people would have punished them and others would have given up on them. "She'll outgrow it and settle down later," some would say. Today we have much more knowledge about how children learn and there are many categories of problems that can be diagnosed. Once diagnosed, teachers can design lessons specifically for a child with a particular learning condition.

In today's world we are requiring only a few skills from children, like sitting still in a classroom, reading, writing, and calculating. In the history of mankind, most children were expected to learn to do things, like fishing or planting vegetables. Maybe they learned crafts like weaving or pottery. These were active things children learned by doing, not by reading a book. The classroom environment isn't the best place for all children to learn. Statistics are vague but estimates currently are that one out of five children needs special help for learning disabilities of some sort to adapt teaching to the child's abilities because they can't function well in a typical classroom.

Other children may need help managing emotional events in their lives. Coping with a divorce or with a death in the family may be helped with counseling. Expert help is also very useful for children who have experienced major trauma, like living in a war zone or a refugee camp.

More and more Muslims are entering the fields of psychology and education so we can more likely find an expert who understands our background when we need help. It is also becoming easier to find specialists who understand Muslim patients, even if they are not Muslim themselves. We turn to Allah in prayer and ask for help. We must not forget to look around us and see what help He has already put within our reach.

Concerning Physical Punishment

People have been hitting children to discipline them all throughout history in cultures all over the world. In the culture of the Arabs before Prophet Muhammad (s), it was commonplace, just like drinking alcohol. We have one sole hadith that mentions hitting a child:

Order your children to pray when they become seven years old, and hit them for it when they become ten years old." (Abu Dawud)

Having heard this hadith, many people believe physical punishment of children is not prohibited in Islam. However, serious scholars who have studied this hadith within the full context of Qur'an and Sunnah have placed several qualifications in interpreting it. They seek to put it in context with many other hadith like the following:

Aisha (r) reported, "Messenger of Allah (s) never hit anyone with his hand, neither a servant nor a woman but of course, he did fight in the Cause of Allah. He never took revenge upon anyone for the wrong done to him, but of course, he exacted retribution for the sake of Allah in case the Injunctions of Allah about unlawful acts were violated. (Riyad as-Salihin, Muslim)

Aisha (r) said, "The Messenger of Allah never hit any of his servants, or wives, and his hand never hit anything." (Ibn Majah, Abu Dawud)

154

Narrated Anas ibn Malik, "I served the Prophet (s) at Medina for ten years. I was a boy. Every task that I did was not according to the desire of my master, but he never said the smallest word of contempt to me nor did he say to me, "Why did you do this?" or "Why did you not do this?"" (Abu Dawud)

He who slaps his slave or beats him, the expiation for it is that he should set him free. (Muslim)

Some scholars, like Dr. Mohamed Elzoghbe and Dr. Ali Gomaa, have thrown out the Abu Dawud hadith about hitting a child for not praying on the basis of chain of narration analysis, issues with vocabulary usage, and conflicts with other, stronger material. But some scholars still refer to it, because it mentions when to teach salah and gives some age guidelines.

A number of scholars have said no child under the age of ten should be struck since that is the age mentioned. That restriction alone would force parents to practice other management skills for years and have habits that make hitting not enter their minds as an option. Since the hadith is about salah, some scholars have said the only excuse for hitting should be for something very important, like salah.

There are actually several variations of this hadith, with slightly different wording. *"Teach them salah at seven years old and oblige them at ten years old." (Bayhaqi and Ahmed)* Since salah is not required of children until puberty, some scholars feel these hadiths are the correct versions and the Abu Dawud version is a corrupted one.

For those scholars who do accept the word "hit" in the text of Abu Dawud, they have agreed that the main purpose of hitting would be to demonstrate to the child the seriousness of his mistake and his parent's displeasure. It is not intended to hurt so much as to embarrass the child with the knowledge that his parent had to resort to this most serious step. When it is used only on rare occasions by a parent who is normally kind and in control, it should have a very strong impact.

Pulling from a wide range of hadith, these scholars have agreed that if a child is to be hit:

- Do not hit the face, head, or tender parts of the body.
- Do not hit hard enough to leave a mark on the skin.
- Do not hit when you feel you might lose control.

Some have also added that if you don't think this step will do any good, don't do it.

When all of the discussion of the hadith is studied, it makes sense that the best action would be to follow the example of Prophet Muhammad (s) from the other hadiths mentioned above in this section and not hit any child.

There will always be the parent who says, "You've never met MY child. He just won't respond to anything but hitting." This parent has trained their child that way, often over years of yelling and hitting the child. It will take a lot of effort to retrain the parent in how to manage his or her child, and then get the child on board. It won't happen overnight. Professional help is often needed.

Amna has 3 children, Susan age 11, Adam age 9, and Mina age 6. Amna often feels overwhelmed by the job of caring for them. Like her mother before her, she follows a pattern of yelling orders at the kids a few times, and then, if she doesn't get a fast enough reaction, she slams something on a table or hits something close to the children to make a loud noise. Her next step is to lunge at one of the kids and wave her hand in the direction of the child. Generally she misses, because the child moves away quickly. But often she ends up slapping the child. Her children are used to this pattern. But Amna noticed long ago that her system isn't very good. Susan is defiant and talks back to her mother. Adam just closes himself off and avoids her all the time. Mina starts crying easily and her teacher at school has confronted Amna about it.

Finally Amna decides to try controlling her anger and stop the yelling. She has read some books on parenting and child development and has friends who are encouraging her. They know she yells at her kids but they don't know about the hitting. She doesn't think of herself as abusive and she'd deny it if anyone asked her about it or accused her. She rationalizes that she has a "little problem with her temper." If the kids get slapped, it's because they didn't move fast enough. She is so in denial that she would say it is their fault, not hers, if they get hit "by mistake."

For the first few days, things go calmly. She asks her children to do things using her most polite voice. There is some compliance but the children seem a bit nervous. They don't understand and feel something is wrong. Susan picks a fight deliberately with her mom, yelling at her and trying to make her mom yell back. Will Mom return to normal? Then Mina deliberately drops her milk on the floor and starts crying, standing still in the mess she created. Amna starts yelling at both of them. Adam just goes to his room and closes the door. Yes, things are back to normal.

The cyclic nature of the relationship makes it very hard to change. Amna ignores her children most of the time. Yes, she follows the schedule of their lives, making sure that their laundry and meals are prepared, they get to school on time, and they do homework. But she doesn't really talk to them. Then something sets her off and she yells and hits. The kids behave for a bit. She relaxes for a while, but then goes back to ignoring the children again. And the cycle continues.

This parent needs a lot of patience and courage to change, but the changed relationship with the children will be worth it. Insha Allah. And the children will hopefully learn how to be better parents so it will impact the grandchildren as well Insha Allah. It is good that Amna has friends who have some idea of her problem and are supportive, but she needs classes or counseling in behavior management to overcome her engrained habits and get out of this destructive cycle.

7 - FAMILY

Family relationships are called silat ar-rahm in Arabic, the ties of the womb. The root form of rahm, 'womb', is also the root of the words rahman and raheem, meaning mercy, compassion. We are all family, and the emotions of that connection, are contained in the understanding of Rahman and Raheem, Allah's names.

"The word 'Ar-Rahm' (womb) derives its name from Ar-Rahman (one of the names of Allah) and Allah said, 'I will keep good relations with the one who keeps good relations with you, (womb i.e. relatives) and sever relations with him who will sever relations with you. (Bukhari)

We live in a cultural period where family relationships are often being torn apart so this is difficult today. Economic and career objectives are dominant considerations in many of our life choices. Individual empowerment has also separated many families. The high rate of divorce has also had a big impact. Many people live alone today and create groups of friends, but they have very limited relationships with family members.

But Allah created the relationships of family and commanded us to care for them. He knows exactly who He caused us to be related to. We need to respect these ties, no matter how challenging or difficult they may be.

Among the many verses of Qur'an and hadith are these:

And it is He who created man from water, and then established relationships of lineage and marriage; and your Lord is All-Powerful. (Qur'an 25:54)

Then what would happen if you (hypocrites) were put in charge? Would you cause disorder in the land and betray your family ties? These are (the kinds of people) whom Allah has cursed. He's deafened them and blinded them (from ever understanding anything). (Qur'an 47:22)

Whoever loves that he be granted more wealth and that his lease of life be prolonged, then he should keep good relations with his kinfolks. (Bukhari)

Obviously, it is our adult relationships that shape the child's relationships, because a child cannot form ties with his relatives (at least until his own adulthood) if his parents cut them off or engage in prolonged battles with them. Consequently, if we do not observe our obligations toward our kin, this is not just a personal matter, but it concerns our children and others as well. Moreover, children have less self-control, wisdom, tact, and understanding than adults. If we cannot keep good ties with our family members, either because we don't feel the need or don't know how, or for any other reason, how can we expect our children to learn and respect their obligations? After all, children learn first from our example, then from our words.

The most important first thing we can do for our relationships with our family, and actually with everyone else in our lives, is to work on adopting the Islamic code of ethics, the manners and moral character of a Muslim. And the most important issue here is controlling our speech. This topic alone deserves a whole book or a series of workshops designed to the task of improving our character.

A man who is known for his good character has the same status as someone who stands at night in prayer. (Al-Adab Al-Mufrad, Bukhari)

It is good to avoid backbiting and slander and making derogatory jokes. These goals are very hard for people who were raised in an environment where such talk is standard fare. It encourages us to publicize all the worst things about people and work toward our own self-fulfillment without concern for others. When we live in this kind of environment, covering people's faults can seem like dishonesty, even though Allah considers it a virtue. Being tactful can seem weak, like not standing up for truth and justice.

The Messenger of Allah (s) said to his companions, "Do you know what backbiting is?" They said, "Allah and His Messenger know best." He said, "Backbiting is you talking about your brother in a way he does not like." It was said to him, "What is your view about this if I find what I mentioned in my brother?" He said, "If what you claim is found in him, you have backbitten him, while if that is not in him, it is a slander." (Muslim)

The strong emotions that are called up when we try to change ourselves require a real struggle for us. The first steps in changing ourselves can make us feel really uncomfortable. There are stages in creating personal change. We don't change ourselves overnight. There is a lot of backsliding as we take one step forward and then feel uncomfortable as we try to impose new habits on ourselves. It's so much easier to simply complain about others and how they aren't changing than to change ourselves. So it's important to take small steps and work gradually.

"Take up good deeds only as much as you are able, for the best deeds are those done regularly even if they are few." (Ibn Majah)

"Do good deeds properly, sincerely and moderately. . .Always adopt a middle, moderate, regular course, whereby you will reach your target (of paradise)." (Bukhari)

Our relatives may or may not have good morals and good manners, but that never excuses our behavior. Islam is not a religion for hermits. The first Muslims lived with their families and neighbors and worked to follow Islam faithfully in that environment.

The joiner (of ties of relationship) is not the one who (merely) returns (the good done to him by his relatives), but rather the joiner is the one who, when a relationship is cut, mends it. (Bukhari)

Joining ties is highly recommended and cutting ties is highly discouraged in Islam. When we read the stories of the companions of the Prophet (s), we hear many examples of the problems they had with their families.

Thinking from the perspective of the importance of having our families in our lives, Muslims should view where they decide to live, not just considering where they can earn the most money, but also where they can help their family best.

One man graduated from university and was given a choice of great jobs in a country with an excellent standard of living. But his parents had died and he had younger sisters who were not through school yet living in their home country, which had many economic problems. Because of visa issues, he can't bring his sisters to live with him in the new country he loves. If he can get a reasonable job back home and look after his sisters there, Allah will reward him for his sacrifice. If he has a relative who accepts to take care of his sisters, perhaps he can take one of the great jobs and send money to support the girls. Would the girls be comfortable and well cared for by the relative? Maybe in the future he can help them come for higher education in his new country and they could be with him then. However circumstances work out, he has a responsibility before Allah for his younger sisters and he needs to make plans that arrange for them as well as for him.

With the concern Muslims have to care for their parents and the elderly in the family, placing them in a nursing home or leaving them alone far away from family are rarely acceptable solutions, except when extreme circumstances demand. We should look for houses that allow extended family to live together or find places near us, so they have some independence but we can be around to help them as needed.

Maria and Muhammad are both looking for jobs as they graduate and plan for their wedding. Muhammad's family is spread out all over. His parents are divorced and they live in neighboring towns. His two sets of grandparents live a thousand miles away from his parents, but in the same town with some of his extended family. Maria's hometown and family are near Muhammad's grandparents. If there are reasonable jobs in all places, the best place might be somewhere near Muhammad's grandparents and Maria's family.

While praising the value of living near family, we need to balance the praise with practical thinking. Our religion is one of moderation in all things, and living near family is no exception. When we have the economic means, there is nothing wrong with living across the street or across town rather than all under one roof. Life is less stressful when we have space. We don't have to see our family members every day. The requirement to respect family ties means we should be there to celebrate each other's successes and to support each other when there are troubles. But we have some independence as well. We shouldn't be so distant that a cousin can't tell us he has cancer and needs some help with his children. When a parent becomes disabled, the burden shouldn't fall on one member of the family who lives close while the others excuse themselves because they live far.

No matter where we live, we need to see how we can join ties with our family members, not just parents and brothers and sisters, but the extended family as well. There are some family members it is easy to be friendly with. These are the people with whom we already have good ties. We want to be with them even if we can't for some reason. We phone them, send them photos, and include them in our plans. All that comes naturally and we should make efforts to continue those wonderful ties. But families always have some members who cause us difficulties in some way. These members usually fall into the category of challenging, but a few might actually be dangerous to be around.

Challenging family members come in a wide variety. There are those who make mean, spiteful comments or find ways to belittle others. There is the super-helpful aunt who inserts herself into whatever someone is doing and sweetly makes a task take twice as long. Then there are the in-laws who want everything done their way as though the other side of the family doesn't exist. Dealing with challenging relatives is often an issue of reframing the problem.

Tamara's sister-in-law doesn't fit into the family well. She is often late to events and makes her husband and children late as well. She is eager to bring a dish to a family dinner but always proposes dishes that don't fit the general menu and she has several times arrived when all the other food is ready to serve, but she brought the uncooked ingredients to make a dish that will need to bake an hour in the oven.

If Tamara and the other women of the family distance themselves from this woman, their children will not see each other much. The cousins won't have years of playing together and Tamara's brother will be isolated from his family. If she and other members of the family decide to overlook this woman's difficulties with being on time, the family can have good relations with everyone else.

The sister-in-law will likely notice she is out of step and will make some efforts to correct herself if she feels people haven't already labeled her and rejected her. It may take a few years, but people naturally try to fit into social groups. Over time, Tamara may find a dessert the woman likes to bring that won't upset the menu and won't disrupt the event if it arrives late. She can ask the woman to bring it as a special request. Over time, Tamara may also find her sister-in-law has other talents. Is she great at organizing games with the children? Does she love to babysit and becomes the daycare home for someone in the family? Maybe she is very patient and willing to help care for Aunt Lily, who has dementia.

If we overlook one thing a person does, we can often find something to like about them. When we do it for Allah, He will reward us for it, for joining family ties or supporting the community over our own personal feelings. If we never find something we personally like in a person, maybe we can see that others appreciate them. Someone can be very challenging to one member of the family but be an enjoyable relative to other members of the family.

Dariya's mother-in-law doesn't come to visit very often, but when she comes, she stays about a month and she brings candy enough to destroy the kids' appetites every day of her visit. The rest of the time she just seems to sit around and read Qur'an and watch TV. Dariya has so much to do keeping the children to their schedules of school and homework, playdates and sports activities, plus her job and cooking nicer meals since her mother-in-law is present. All that candy just irritates her and upsets her plans for providing healthy meals for her family. Her husband buries himself in his work but tries to take his mother visiting or out to walk in the nearby parks which she likes to do. He tried to say something about the candy but didn't get anywhere because he's worried about offending his mother, even though he agrees with his wife. A modern, frank conversation about how "this is our house and this is what we insist on for our kids" might feel very cold and insulting to this older woman who raised her son successfully and has lots of experience with family life.

Most older relatives like to give candy to children because it gets the children to pay attention to them. Older people who come to visit are entering a place where children already have routines. Children don't usually sit around visiting with them much. They run around playing or they are off to school. But nothing gives a grandparent more pleasure than to interact with their grandchild.

If Dariya could encourage her children to do things with their grandmother, it might change the dynamic of the visit. They can run errands for her. They can show her their school work. They can tell her about their school day. She can go to watch their sports workouts and maybe their games. She can also be invited to join in any activities around the house.

Parents have the habit of bearing all their parental responsibilities. Having another relative in the house can be the opportunity to shed a few responsibilities to that relative. This can make an older person feel useful and respected, if the request for help is handled diplomatically and not like the parents are using them as maids. A relative can be a good babysitter so parents can take a night out. While a visiting mother is an honored guest, she is also family and should be included in the family routine, helping out and being helped out, not stuck in a guest room and the living room. If Dariya includes her mother-in-law in the family affairs, they can discuss meals and diets in a relaxed way, and Grandma will likely agree with her that the children should have healthy meals and limited candy.

Maybe Grandma doesn't feel welcome in Dariya's kitchen. Encourage her to cook some of her recipes. Her son knows some he can request. Encourage the children to try them. Make her feel welcome and appreciated for her efforts. This can lead to discussions of food and likes and dislikes in the family. She can probably adapt some of her dishes if necessary or remember other, less common dishes she knows how to make that may be more appreciated than her first efforts. The point is to include her in the family so she isn't just sitting around, waiting for someone to notice her and entertain her.

Can she tell stories? Maybe she can entertain the dinner table with stories of growing up and how different things were then? Maybe she can go through a photo album with the children and talk about family memories? She might be better at helping her grandson with his math homework than his mother, who often loses patience.

Then there are the relatives who are not just challenging, but they have habits that are against Islam, so we need to protect our children and other members of the family, while keeping ties.

Mahmut's Uncle Isa owns a grocery store in a poor neighborhood where he sells beer, other alcohol, lottery tickets, cigarettes, and groceries.

Mahmut can protect his family from his uncle by keeping them away from the store and avoiding conversation about the business. In this way he is covering the faults of his uncle, while allowing him to have positive relationships with his family. And his aunt and the children of his uncle will have positive relationships with his family, too.

When the topic comes up, as it will from time to time, he can comment to his children that the store is selling bad products, and much of the income is not halal. But there is no reason to dwell on the problem. Maybe in the future, Allah will reveal a way to change the business of his uncle but it is blocked for now.

"Whoever believes in Allah and the Last Day, should serve his guest generously; and whoever believes in Allah and the Last Day, should unite the bond of kinship (i.e. keep good relations with his relatives); and whoever believes in Allah and the Last Day, should say what is good or keep quiet." (Bukhari)

A bigger problem for Mahmut is Uncle Amin. He is considered the head of the family and is very proud of the family history he can recite going back generations. He interferes with plans different members of the family want to make for all sorts of things, particularly marriage and education. He bullies people to get his way. His daughter Fatima disobeyed him and went to nursing school. He thinks nursing is menial work and not good enough for his children. He cut her off from the family.

Uncle Isa does wrong things, but he keeps quiet about it. It is easy to cover his faults in front of the family. Uncle Amin hurts members of the family, with his un-Islamic teachings and advice. This needs specific efforts to isolate him and reduce his power, while still respecting the man. It isn't necessary to have a public fight with him, but Mahmut can encourage other family members to disregard Uncle Amin's advice. He can arrange occasions for Fatima to join the family for some events. He can limit the time his children have with this man and make sure to politely address the problems with Uncle Amin's advice and stories of family history. He needs to speak clearly to his children about his goals for their future careers and spouses and stress that they can please him even if they don't please Uncle Amin. If he remains silent on these things, it could be understood by his children that he agrees with his uncle.

Don't puff up your cheek (arrogantly) at other people nor strut around through the earth, for Allah has no love for conceited snobs. (Qur'an 31:18)

Allah, Most High, has removed from you the pride of the pre-Islamic period and its boasting of ancestors. One is only a pious believer or a miserable sinner. You are children of Adam, and Adam came from dust... (Abu Dawud, Tirmidhi)

Some people might say this is two-faced, if Mahmut is polite to his uncle while actively working to minimize the damage the man does in the family. But in Islam, we respect the person Allah created and separate the person from the deeds of the person. Uncle Amin will grumble and complain about people not following his advice and Mahmut must act with diplomacy and tact. But we don't follow advice that is against our faith.

There is nothing wrong with children learning their family history. But stories of past relatives can be interpreted in different ways. Suppose a great-grandfather was a noted scholar of Islam, a sheikh. The family can be proud of that but it doesn't mean family members are superior to other people. That would be arrogance, and the hadith of the Prophet is that someone who is arrogant won't enter Paradise. It should be an inspiration to children that they can try to be good scholars themselves. Some children, particularly if they find difficulty in some aspect of Islamic scholarship, like memorizing Qur'an, may feel themselves unworthy of their relative and stop trying. So parents need to use the stories of important ancestors tactfully.

There are people who trace their lineage back to Prophet Muhammad. If this is a source of inspiration to encourage them to follow Islam more carefully, it may be helpful to them. We are each accountable for our own deeds no matter what our parentage is.

No bearer of burdens can bear the burden of another (Qur'an, 17:15)

If there are relatives who have passed away who did bad things, we should cover their faults. This means simply not talking about them or at least not talking about the bad they did. Sometimes the common knowledge of wrongdoing circulates and children learn about bad things.

A mother might need to tell her children, "Yes, your father died from a gunshot wound when he was trying to rob a store. He was suffering from a drug addiction. Drug addiction causes people to make poor choices and do bad things. When he wasn't under the influence, he was a very kind person who loved me and you. I remember the fun times we had before the addiction robbed him from me." She can show photos of the happy times with their father and talk of that. And she can educate the children about the dangers of addiction so they will hopefully avoid it.

Do not abuse the dead, for they have surely reached what they sent on ahead. (Bukhari)

"Whoever conceals the (hidden) fault of his Muslim brother, Allah (swt) will conceal his faults on the Day of Resurrection. Whoever exposes the fault of his Muslim brother, Allah will expose his faults, until He shames him, due to it, in his (own) house." (Ibn Majah)

"Whoever relieves a Muslim of a burden from the burdens of the world, Allah will relieve him of a burden from the burdens on the Day of Judgement. And whoever helps ease a difficulty in the world, Allah will grant him ease from a difficulty in the world and in the Hereafter. And whoever covers (the faults of) a Muslim, Allah will cover (his faults) for him in the world and the Hereafter. And Allah is engaged in helping the worshipper as long as the worshipper is engaged in helping his brother." (Tirmidhi)

Sometimes there is a relative who is too dangerous to be around and it is necessary to stop seeing them to keep safe. Sometimes, to hide from a relative who has control issues and threatens violence, it is necessary to stop communicating with other relatives who continue to have relations with that person. We don't cut ties completely, but we limit relationships as much as possible for protection, until the need for protection is over.

It is good for someone to consult with others before taking this step. Maybe mediation can solve the problem or make it less dangerous. Consulting others also helps a person avoid falling victim to fear. Is the situation bad enough to require leaving? What is the best way to handle the relationship safely? On the other hand, the people we consult may not understand the problem and the extent of the danger. Abusive people, dangerous people, don't change in a day or even a month. And they can be very pleasant much of the time. Physical abuse is usually unplanned, and abusers have poor control of their impulses so they can attack spontaneously, even if an hour before they swore they would never hit again. They will argue it is the fault of their victim for triggering their impulse, rather than accepting responsibility for their own lack of self-control. Worse perhaps are the people who obsess on revenge, stalking their victim and planning their attack. Psychological abuse is a mindset, a whole way of thinking about how people interact with the world. The person interprets what others say and do in a way that justifies for himself or herself a right to be mean to them. Changing thinking patterns takes a long time and effort. If they don't seek counseling and really work on changing themselves, they might never change.

Some of the early Muslims moved to Medina precisely to avoid relatives who threatened them for converting. We all have a right, and even a duty, to protect ourselves and our children from abusive and dangerous relationships.

A woman married a man from a different cultural background from hers, even though they were both Muslim, and they had lots of fights. He would hit her and scream abusive language at her. They had a son together. After a few years, she got the courage to divorce him and took their little boy to another city where she got a job and established herself. To protect herself, since her ex-husband was harassing her with threats, particularly to take their small son from her, she didn't tell anyone from her old home where she had gone.

She told her new friends she had left an abusive relationship. When the son was in high school, she died of cancer and the people of her town were concerned about where to place her son. She had told them her ex-husband was horrible and she wanted her son to stay away from him. Several families offered the boy a home, but leaders at the mosque, understanding the requirement not to cut ties, made discrete inquiries about his father, back in the old city. They discovered he had remarried and had other children. His present wife was from his culture and, from all reports they had a reasonable marriage and their children were doing well. They finally contacted the man and told him about his son. He welcomed the boy with open arms into his home, and his wife did as well. The boy had heard only bad about his father from his mother, but he met a different person. He went to live with his father, taking phone numbers of his mother's friends in case he needed help, and established relationships with all his father's family. The boy won't forget his mother and her sacrifices for him. And he may always have some lack of trust in his father. But his father can help him with his education. He can also now have relationships with his half-brothers and sisters and other relatives on his father's side of the family. He will become an independent adult soon anyway and this family support will help him.

This story could have ended with the boy staying with friends in his mother's town until he grew up to go off on his own. It is included here because sometimes people do change, or circumstances change so they behave differently. We need to keep open to that possibility, even though years may pass before someone can renew ties.

If non-Muslim relatives accept having Muslim relatives, and treat them with respect, there are generally no problems with religious differences. Muslims can treat them like regular family members, while still keeping a slight distance where necessary to maintain Muslim identity, like avoiding parties they give where alcohol is served. Problems usually arise for converts or for a Muslim man who marries a non-Muslim woman.

Sandra has been a Muslim for several years. She's married to Musa and they've just had a baby. Her Baptist father disowned her when he learned she'd converted. He would hate her marrying anyone who wasn't Baptist, but this Muslim man is really from Satan in his eyes and he refuses to have any relationship with her. Sandra's mom was raised Catholic. She doesn't want to upset her husband. She has been going to the Baptist church since they got married. So she has been communicating with Sandra without him knowing about it. Her father's relatives who are church-goers treat Sandra like her father does. Her mom's relatives are unsure what this Islam stuff is, but they always loved her so they are willing to put up with it. Sandra sends pictures of the baby to her mom and grandma and they visit, though Sandra's mom makes sure to keep this contact hidden from her father. It's awkward but hopefully as the years go by, her father may mellow his position. He has only heard horrible lies about Islam. Maybe he will meet her husband and children sometime at her grandmother's or at one of her maternal aunts and uncles. Sandra has produced his only grandchild so far, after all. But maybe that relationship will remain blocked no matter how others try to heal it.

There can be trust problems. Sandra has always been close to her grandmother and Grandma loves to babysit. But Sandra's grandmother may take her first great-grandchild to see Santa at the mall. If it feels like Grandma just didn't realize that wasn't right, it may be overlooked. One small issue shouldn't overwhelm all the general good relationship Sandra has with her grandmother. However, if Grandma starts fussing about getting the child baptized or is discovered to be trying to secretly teach the child her faith, Sandra will have to limit the time her child spends with Grandmother and find someone else to babysit who is more trustworthy.

Another problem might be that Grandma doesn't feel Sandra's diet restrictions are important. Surely the child needs to learn to eat BLT sandwiches [BLT is bacon, lettuce and tomato.]. Grandma makes them all the time. Sandra used to love them when she was little. Hopefully Grandma can relearn to make peanut butter and jelly sandwiches, avoiding bacon and ham products, or serve a lunch Sandra prepares for her child. Sandra will need to navigate these issues tactfully and adjust visits politely to ensure her child is protected.

Oh you who believe, don't take those who mock and belittle your way of life as best friends, whether from among those who received a scripture before you or from among those who reject (the truth). Be mindful of Allah if you're true believers. (Qur'an 5:57)

Allah doesn't forbid you, from being kind and fair to those who don't fight you because of your beliefs or drive you from your homes, for Allah loves the tolerant. (Qur'an 60:8)

Asma bint Abu Bakr reported: During the period of the peace treaty of the Quraysh with the Messenger of Allah (s), my mother, accompanied by her father, came to visit me, and she was an idolater. I consulted the Messenger of Allah (s) and said, "Oh Messenger of Allah, my mother has come to me and she desires (what a mother desires from a daughter).

170

Shall I keep good relations with her?" He said. "Yes, keep good relations with her." (Bukhari)

...So be thankful to Me and to your parents, for the final destination (of you all) is back (to Me). However, if (your parents) try to force you to set up partners with Me, offering (deities) about which you know nothing, then don't obey them. Yet, still keep company with them in this world in a fair manner. (Qur'an 31:14-15)

The biggest problem is one of communication and correcting false information. If Sandra's father has cut her off, there is no communication so she and her husband can't correct his understanding of what Islam is about. For him it is all evil. With Sandra's grandmother, and some other relatives, she can invite them to her home, to the aqiqah to celebrate the birth of her child, to Eid [Islamic holiday] celebrations and other events. They can learn how well she and her husband live together with the other Muslims in his family and with the Muslim community.

There will be things they won't like but they may appreciate things Sandra doesn't recognize. At parties Sandra's parents host, people are invited as couples. They are all about the same age as Sandra's parents and Grandma is older, without a spouse. There she never feels like she fits in. At the women's parties Sandra hosts, Grandma doesn't feel out of place when she attends. There are women and girls of all ages and they make her feel welcome.

Hopefully too, as the children get older, Grandma will recognize that they are polite, well-behaved kids. They run errands for her and like to sit and talk to her. The fact that they are Muslim shouldn't prevent them from having a good relationship with her.

Abdul-Haq loves his faith but he also loves Cindy and she's Christian. Though he didn't see the point when they got married, the imam, the religious leader at the mosque, insisted that Cindy agree in their marriage contract, properly witnessed, that she would accept to raise their children Muslim. This should have led them to discuss the issue at that time, but neither one of them was worried about kids back then. Cindy has liked Abdul-Haq's faith practice because it gives their life structure. Now that they have their first child, some problems they hadn't considered have started cropping up.

The first problem was that Cindy's parents put a lot of pressure on them to give the child the name Christopher, after Cindy's grandfather who died a few months before the birth. They finally compromised on Yusuf Ali, after Cindy's other grandfather Joseph and Abdul-Haq's grandfather Ali. Then Cindy's parents wanted a baptism at their church. Cindy finally ended that issue, sort of, by telling them they would wait and see what Yusuf decided himself when he was older. That idea upset Abdul-Haq but he kept quiet because it quieted his in-laws.

Before Yusuf entered middle school though, some marital problems between Cindy and Abdul-Haq got worse and led them to divorce. They agreed on a shared custody program and Cindy agreed to continue taking the kids to the mosque on the weekend for their Islamic education.

Then Cindy met and married a man who is very serious about going to church. He started encouraging Cindy and his step-children to attend with him and his children from a previous marriage. Cindy again appreciates the structure he imposes on life and decides it's good for the children to know a religion that is more mainstream than Islam. Her new husband starts making efforts to convert Yusef and his sister to Christianity. The children aren't happy and complain to their father. Abdul-Haq now discovers the importance of his marriage contract, with Cindy's promise to raise the children Muslim. He uses it to threaten to take custody of his children away from Cindy in court. By this time, Yusuf is in high school and his sister is in middle school. They already have a strong Islamic identity and don't like this stepfather. After months of tense discussion, Abdul-Haq and Cindy agree on a new custody arrangement so the children spend more time with their father, making him the custodial parent, and Cindy and her new husband agree to avoid discussing religion with the children.

People change over time. In the heat of romance, people can agree to all sorts of promises that, ten or twenty years later they may regret. It is best if couples have deep discussions about their future life together before they marry. Marriage counseling is cheaper before marriage than after.

8 – HOLIDAYS AND COMMUNITY

Eid al-Fitr and Eid al-Adha are the two big holidays of Islam. We need to make them important events for our children, as well as for ourselves. From the religious perspective, the important event in each is the large community prayers. In the time of the Prophet (s), these prayers were held outside in a large area that could accommodate the whole town together. No one was excluded. Everyone gathered and joined in the chant that precedes the prayer. After the prayer, they sat to hear the Eid khutbah (speech). Then people turned to greet and congratulate each other for either the community's completion of the fasting of Ramadan or for the success of those members of the community who completed the rites of Hajj.

Zakat al-Fitr, a donation of money for each member of any household that has the means to pay, is collected before Eid al-Fitr, so food and money can be distributed to the poor and they can enjoy the holiday. The qurbani, or sacrifice of an animal, slaughtered for Eid al-Adha, commemorating the practice of Prophet Abraham (s), provides a good meal for both those who do the sacrifice and the poor to whom they distribute much of the meat.

Both holidays are times for family and friends to gather and congratulate each other, giving thanks to Allah (swt) for His many blessings, and sharing with the community so all can be included in the celebration. Each community of Muslims around the world has some customs and food specialties that they created to make these holidays special and adapt them to the places where they live. New converts and people living in new areas need to create their own ways of celebrating. For our children, we need to show them that our holidays are as fun and enjoyable as the holidays of other people who live around us.

Where people have the means to do it, many Muslim communities are organizing amusement activities, with inflatable bounce houses and zip-lines, pony rides, slides, and other things that can be set up outside a mosque or inside a large hall where the Eid prayer takes place. Some communities organize a large picnic at a public park or community center for everyone to join in a big meal together. They may hire a clown to entertain the children and organize other activities near the picnic. Some groups of families arrange to meet up in activity centers that are available in their town, like a local bowling alley or skating place, where they can all play together. Competing somewhat with Christmas in America, Eid has become a time of fancier gifts for children than the traditional few pieces of candy or pocket money.

There can be activities for children in the home as well. In addition to helping clean the house, children can help preparing any special meals and desserts the family might enjoy. Children can make decorations to hang around the house and do other art projects. Families also involve them in planning any celebrations they want to do after the prayers. Children should also be encouraged to join in contacting and visiting with family members who are distant. With technology today, while children can still make and send cards or little gifts to their grandparents, they can also phone with video and tell them all about what they have been doing.

While they are not holidays, there are several other occasions celebrated in different parts of the Muslim world. Some people commemorate the hijra, the first day of Muharram, a month on the Islamic calendar. It's about the time the Prophet (s) left Makkah for Madinah and established the Muslim community there on the invitation of the people of Madinah.

In some places people celebrate the Prophet's birthday, (Mawlid an-Nabi). The exact date of his birth is unknown, and the celebration is very low-key compared to Christmas. People simply have small parties where they review the Prophet's life story and remind themselves of his importance in their lives. Mosques may have the Friday khutbah cover the same topic as well.

On Isra and Miraj, (also known as Lailat al-Miraj), the night of the Prophet's journey to Heaven and back, and Lailat al-Qadr, the Night of Power, when the first revelation of the Qur'an happened, many Muslims stay up all or part of the night to pray. During Ramadan, there are special taraweeh prayers each evening after 'isha prayer (the night prayer). They can be prayed in congregation at a mosque or at home.

There are special days for fasting, like Mondays and Thursdays, or the middle three days of each lunar month, and of course the six days of Shawal. A person who fasts any six days in Shawal, the lunar month which comes right after Ramadan, after completing the fasting of Ramadan, is considered to earn a reward similar to fasting the whole year. Fasting the day of Arafat, when all the people doing Hajj are praying together at Arafat near Mecca, is recommended if a person is not doing Hajj. The following day is Eid al Fitr and fasting on either of the two Eid days is not allowed. Many people fast the day of Ashura, the tenth day of Muharram, because the Prophet valued it. It commemorates the day when Moses and his people were saved from Pharaoh by the parting of the sea. It's also the day when the Prophet's grandson Husain was killed in the Battle of Karbala, so it has a great significance to Shia Muslims as well. Older children can join their parents in these special times for prayer and fasting if they want. These occasions are good to practice if someone has the time and the ability.

In some communities, families celebrate when a child memorizes his or her first surah and again perhaps when the child finishes reading the whole Qur'an in Arabic. Otherwise, Muslims celebrate when good things happen to them, like a wedding, a job promotion, or a graduation. The important guidelines for celebrations are that people thank Allah for the good that has happened to them and share with others, particularly with the poor and less fortunate. These aren't times for showing off but for being grateful. Nothing comes to us except if Allah wills it, and we need to share the good He gives us with others to express our gratitude. Parties should be generous but also stay within the means of the hosts.

Like everyone else in our community, Muslims can also enjoy other activities and celebrations. The American Thanksgiving can be a time for us to join with others in our community to thank God for the successful harvest and spend time with family and friends. If a town celebrates community events such as a Pumpkin Festival or a Frontier Days Festival, we can participate with our children as much as we feel comfortable. It's fun to go see fireworks, watch parades, and picnic with family and friends. We are part of the larger community and we and our children should feel comfortable as members of this community, as long as our religious practices and beliefs are not compromised.

175

New Muslims often have so much internal changing to do that they may feel a need to withdraw from the larger community for a while, until they feel comfortable with their transition. This may take several years for some people. As one new convert remarked, "Who am I as a Muslim? Normally I'd have a beer with my old friends while watching the fireworks. It feels weird to attend and just awkward to sit away from them." But gradually they adapt and can return when they feel comfortable. It's like a child participated in community activities, left as a teen, and then came back as an adult with a different perspective and responsibility and rejoined the community.

There are many community activities today that are interfaith in nature, specifically designed to be inclusive of people of diverse faiths. Prayer breakfasts, civil rights demonstrations, and political demonstrations are among the activities we can all participate in with others in the larger community. Our children can join us and it is important that they see us show them how to be active citizens, part of the larger whole of our nation. This helps them feel that they are not marginalized, that Muslims count here and that Muslims should be active civically and they can make a difference in the life of the country.

Our life in this society automatically exposes us and our children to a variety of non-Muslim holidays and occasions. It is nice that people generally try to include everyone in these celebrations today, but there are a few we need to keep at arm's length and some we need to avoid altogether. The commercialization of holidays in the United States has resulted in a marketing assault on everyone. Christmas is the worst offender with Halloween growing to a close second. Stores are filled with displays. Holiday music, films, videos, and other media formats saturate the community for weeks at a time. Our children can be entertained and attracted to all of this, as we might be ourselves, particularly if we are converts.

Different families handle these issues in different ways, depending on their circumstances. Some just stay home a lot and stay away from media sources. This is a very relaxing way to manage. But children do go to school and we do have to do some shopping. Schools have been navigating the changes in society gradually over the past fifty or so years, as Protestant prayer in school was removed and religious music and art projects have gradually been replaced with other themes. Parents still need to discuss the issues of holidays with teachers and sometimes with school administrators.

The first six years of a child's life are the years when children learn their basic identity. This identity will usually stay with the child as a default setting for his or her life. Children learn their names, who their family is, their gender, ethnic identity, religious identity, and nationality. The next several years add details to this identity development within the child. So these are the years when we need to make the most effort to avoid confusion for the child. The messages from parents and other family members, from the neighbors and other community members and from all the diverse media exposure children face, all come together inside the child to tell the child who he or she is supposed to be in life. If we can arrange a consistent, coherent message for our children most of the time, particularly in their younger years, we can expect them to have a strong, confident sense of themselves and their identity as they grow into adulthood and find their place in the workforce and society.

So we need to model confidence and clear values for our children. Make sure our children only eat healthy, halal food at school, from their earliest days there. Keep them home from school for Muslim holidays, the two Eids, even if the school doesn't recognize them. Schools should have the Eids on their calendars and recognize them as excused absences. If there are enough Muslims in the school, in some places these are school holidays.

Easter, Valentine's Day, Halloween, and Christmas have all come from the Christian faith. Our children need to learn about all holidays and customs even if we don't participate in celebrating them. Muslim families need to decide how much they want their children to participate in secularized events that may have started as part of a faith tradition but have evolved to the point that it's hard to see the religious origin, like Valentine's Day. We want our children to develop a strong identity as Muslims but we also want them to feel part of the whole culture around us. We want to protect them from any glamorizing of negative elements in some of these events, too.

Easter is a very important event in the Christian church, the day they celebrate what they believe was the resurrection of Jesus Christ. The Easter bunny and decorated eggs are not part of church teachings. They came from religions practiced by some people before they became Christian and they have been absorbed by popular culture. It was common fifty or sixty years ago in the United States for Christian children to receive new clothes for Easter. There is still an Easter Parade in New York City where everyone is expected to parade in their best clothes on Easter Sunday. Easter egg hunts have been organized as community events in many places. The White House has an Easter Egg Roll event every year.

Saint Valentine is a Catholic saint for engaged couples and happy marriages. Before Valentine's Day cards became a mass-produced, inexpensive item, children made a few valentines as art projects in school and gave them to classmates. This led to some children receiving many valentines and others few or none. Then parents and teachers switched to packets of cards from stores, and children were told to give one to every child in the class. Today this is generally celebrated in early elementary schools as a friendship day.

Halloween is not a church celebration. It is derived from All Hallow's Eve, the evening before All Hallows Day, or All Saint's Day, which is celebrated in the Christian Church. All Saint's Day is their day to remember all of the saints and to visit cemeteries and remember family. The evening, or night, before All Saint's Day was a night of evil, not from church teachings particularly, but from pre-Christian traditions, in some places, tied to earlier faiths. There were customs practiced to protect the house from evil ghosts and other beings. There were people who took this occasion to play mean pranks on neighbors or engage in vandalism during the night. Over time, all of this has been transformed into the secular event practiced today. People dress up in costumes and have parties. Children dress in costumes and have a limited time in the early evening to walk through their neighborhood and ask neighbors for candy. Schools have costume parties. The themes of evil, including witchcraft and ghosts, are the most worrisome parts of this occasion.

Christmas for converts to Islam can pose issues. They may have Christian relatives or non-religious family who celebrate the holiday with all the trimmings. Plus, particularly for newer converts, Christmas often holds strong emotional ties. It is a whole month of decorating, fun, music, and the excitement of preparing presents for others. People who remember their childhood anticipation of Santa and guessing about gifts under a beautiful tree can have a lot of emotional issues giving all that up. It takes time.

It can be helpful for a new convert to think of the holiday in its parts and pieces and decide what parts are easy to give up and what parts are very meaningful and will be particularly missed. With the parts that will be hard to give up, what can the person do as a Muslim that will have a similar feeling? For example, some people love decorating the house. It makes the house look special. These people might enjoy planning decorations for the Eids and making their homes feel special at those times.

Muslim converts often give gifts to their parents, and maybe another relative or so, who would be badly hurt if they were forgotten. The intention of the gift is to show love to a relative who might otherwise feel hurt. And if grandma insists on giving Christmas gifts to her Muslim grandchildren, they can accept them graciously, but we don't need to encourage it. Hopefully grandma can move beyond this, particularly if we include her in our Eid celebrations and she sees the kids get presents then.

Allah's Messenger (s) used to accept gifts and used to give something in return. (Bukhari)

Give gifts, for indeed the gift removes bad feelings from the chest. And let the neighbor not look down upon (the gift of) her neighbor, even if it be the lower shanks of sheep. (Tirmidhi)

However, this applies only as long as there are no "strings" attached to receiving a gift. The Prophet (s) also said,

Oh people, accept presents so long as they remain presents. But when the Quraysh [leaders of Mecca who were not Muslim] quarrel about the rule, and the presents are given for the religion of one of you [to bribe you away from Islam], then leave them alone. (Abu Dawud)

179

We do need to politely draw a line of distinction between ourselves and our relatives of other faiths. It's generally best to avoid the Christmas morning gift-opening scene and all the Santa story, although our children should know about Christmas in the same way Christian children should know about our Eids. Some Christian families have foods and alcohol in their celebrations that we need to avoid. They may have home prayer activities, like a blessing they always say with some ceremony, before their Christmas dinner. If they accommodate us, we can join in family gatherings with them as we ask them to join in our family social gatherings at our Eids.

Some converts may have family from faiths other than Christian. They need to examine how their families practice their faiths in a similar manner. We don't want to participate in faith practices of others but we want to maintain good relationships with our families where we can. We don't invite them to our Eid prayers but we can invite them to our social events after the prayers, if they would like to attend. We don't go to their prayer services but we might be able to attend their social family gatherings if they can accommodate our food requirements.

One thing we don't want is for our family to feel upset that they are accommodating us. If Mom really wants to make us feel welcome and come to her home for Christmas dinner, maybe other members of the family will be upset that she won't serve wine with the meal, because of us, or that Dad says a simple blessing at the table that doesn't invoke Jesus Christ. We don't want to cause problems. This might be one of the situations where one person is upset if we don't come and another is upset if we do. Family dynamics can make this a difficult issue to navigate. Talking out the possible problems with different family members well in advance may be a better strategy than having them find their holiday celebration has been modified by others without telling them.

Birthday celebrations bring some special issues. The custom of celebrating birthdays was initiated to celebrate the births of the royal and noble children of Europe. Gradually the celebration of birthdays worked its way down to the middle class, until it became an occasion for all people. It has never been a Muslim tradition. Following the Muslim tradition for celebrations, if a person wants to celebrate his thanks for having lived some number of years of life, it should be by giving a party for others, not by expecting others to shower him with gifts.

However, in many communities, our children will be socially isolated if they can't go to birthday parties while all their friends give them and have them. Birthdays are an event parents often use to teach children how to have a party and use manners. Children learn how to be inclusive in their friend list for the party. Where Muslim children have few other social activities, their parents often let them participate in these birthday rituals, while trying to keep things modest and low-key. We can avoid birthdays in many situations and downplay them in others. Gift-giving should be simple. Some people encourage gifts to charity instead of personal ones.

We have community activities with Muslims that hopefully will be very meaningful for our children. We also have activities with the larger community that can be fun and meaningful or educational. We are members of that larger community with all the rights, privileges, and responsibilities as anyone else and we have a lot of flexibility in deciding what we want to participate in and when we want to withdraw. We want our children to have a strong sense of belonging both to the Muslim community and to the land where we live.

9 – THE BIRTH OF A BABY

Muslims have five traditions to carry out on the birth of a baby. These are all things the Prophet Muhammad (s) did or ordered to be done and are documented in hadith. They are considered Sunnah, following the example of the Prophet, but not fard (obligatory). The two strongest traditions are saying the adhan in the ear of the newborn and circumcision for boys. These two are almost universally done.

Adhan (call to prayer)

If one has a baby and makes the adhan in its right ear and the iqamah (call to line up for prayer) in its left ear, Satan will not disturb the child, Allah willing. (Baihaqi)

I saw the Messenger of Allah say the adhan in the ear of Al-Hasan bin Ali - when he was born to Fatima. (Tirmidhi, Abu Dawud)

We do this shortly after the birth of a baby. Anyone can do it. Many parents consider this an honor and ask someone special to perform the act for their child.

Aqiqah (celebration for the newborn)

Every child... is ransomed *by his aqiqah, which is done on the seventh day.* (Tirmidhi, al-Nasa'i, Ibn Majah)

With the aqiqah we thank Allah for His blessing in giving us this child and we announce the birth to our community. The concept of 'ransom' mentioned in the hadith refers to the ransom of the son of Prophet Ibrahim (Abraham) (s) who sacrificed a ram instead of his child. The aqiqah is a practice from the Sunnah of Prophet Ibrahim (s). Like he did with the practice of Hajj, also from the Sunnah of Prophet Ibrahim (s), Prophet Muhammad (s) ordered his followers to continue the practice.

The examples from the time of the Prophet show people hosting feasts according to the traditions of their times and their economic ability. The child is a blessing from Allah so we should make a sacrifice for him or her to express our gratitude. In sharing food with others in the community, we help strengthen it. If someone receives meat or food from an aqiqah, that person should pray for the child so this provides more protection for the child.

Today, families can adapt this Sunnah to the customs of their area and their ability. Not everyone eats lamb or can afford it but everyone knows how to have a feast and celebrate.

Traditionally the lamb meat is shared, one third for the family, one third for friends, and one third for the poor, but all of it can be given to the poor. The family can invite all the neighborhood, rich and poor, to the feast. If the aqiqah is delayed for practical reasons, like concern for the mother's health, or to wait until family can come together for the occasion, that's fine. The name of the baby was announced to the community at the aqiqah, like people sending out birth announcements today. The name can be selected at any time before the formal announcement.

If anyone has a child born to him and wishes to offer a sacrifice on its behalf, he may offer two sheep resembling each other for a boy and one for a girl. (Abu Dawud)

This hadith is often quoted. But the Prophet didn't follow his own advice for his grandsons. In fact, hadith have minor differences in details of these Sunnah events.

It is reported that the Messenger of Allah sacrificed a sheep on the seventh day for his grandsons Husain and Hasan and instructed the boy's mother, his daughter Fatimah, to shave the baby's head and give the weight of his hair in silver as sadaqah (charity). (Muwatta, Abu Dawud)

Imam Malik wrote in his book on hadith, Muwatta, "What we do about the aqiqah is that if someone makes an aqiqah for his children, he gives a sheep for both male and female. The aqiqah is not obligatory but it is desirable to do it…"

The Prophet said, "A child is ransomed by his aqiqah. Sacrifice is made for him on the seventh day, his head is shaved, and he is given a name." (Abu Dawud)

Some people might consider shaving the baby's head a sixth Sunnah. Some just consider it a part of the aqiqah, along with slaughtering an animal to share its meat. There is no separate party for shaving the baby's head, or any ceremony. People just do it at home in any safe way. It is normal for babies to lose their initial hair and new hair grows in. This shaving can help keep the baby clean from slowly shedding hair. Some babies have hardly any hair at birth. If parents don't see enough to bother shaving, remember this is a Sunnah and not an obligation. The parent might just clip a few hairs with the scissors and give a small donation to charity in remembrance of this custom. The weight of hair is usually not substantial in any case and the amount of silver it represents is usually a small amount.

Fatima, the daughter of the Messenger of Allah (s), weighed the hair of Hasan, Husain, Zaynab, and Umm Kulthum, and gave away in sadaqa an equivalent weight of silver. (Muwatta)

Tahneek

This is a simple thing to do for a newborn. People soften a date and rub it gently on the palate (upper part of the mouth) of the baby. The dates used for this are soft and rather sticky anyway. This only gives the baby a bit of the taste but no part of the date is left in the baby's mouth that might cause a choking risk. There is no particular time for doing this but traditionally people do it soon after the birth if they are going to do it.

A son was born to me and I took him to the Prophet, who named him Ibrahim, did tahneek for him with a date, invoked Allah to bless him, and returned him to me. (Muslim)

Aisha reported that the new-born infants were brought to Allah's Messenger (s). He blessed them and rubbed their palates with dates. (Muslim)

In some places dates may not be available or only very dry hard dates may be found. It is Sunnah and not a required act. There are several hadith that say people brought their newborns to present to the Prophet and he did this for the baby and sometimes also gave the baby a name. This is, in a way, a little "gift" to the baby.

Tasmiyah (naming)

The Prophet (s) not only was asked by parents to give names to their children but he also changed the names of some of the people who came to say *shahadah*. Several hadiths relate to naming a child.

On the Day of Resurrection, you will be called by your names and by your fathers' names, so give yourselves good names. (Abu Dawud)

Based on the examples of naming by the Prophet, scholars give the following advice concerning the giving of a name:

- Names shouldn't be too proud, like Malik al-Mulk (the King of Kings). (Muslim, Abu Dawud).
- Names shouldn't be identified with another faith or indicate allegiance to anyone but Allah. So Abd ar Rahman is good, because it means servant of The All Merciful, one of the names of Allah, but Abd ur Rasul would not be because it means servant of the prophet. All names where Abd comes before one of the names of Allah are good names. Names like Christopher (after St. Christopher, or any name from the calendar of Catholic saints) or Lakshmi (a Hindu goddess) should not be used.
- Names of the prophet, including Jesus, are good because they attach a good example to the child.
- Names should give the child a good sense about him/herself. They shouldn't be embarrassing or ugly.
- Names do not have to be Arabic names.

Khitan (circumcision)

The Prophet said: The practices related to fitra are five: circumcision, shaving the pubic hair, trimming the mustache, cutting the nails, and removing the underarm hair. (Bukhari, Muslim, Muwatta)

There is no mention of circumcision in the Qur'an. It is in hadith. Al-Baihaqi says it was done for baby boys about the same time as the aqiqah. It is not a sign of a special relationship to Allah, like the Jews make it but it is a practice started by Prophet Ibrahim (s), the ancestor of both religions. While it is not a fard, (obligation) it is extremely close to being

185

one. Scholars have made exceptions for older men who convert to Islam and certainly any unusual health risk is an exception.

Circumcision is part of respecting the fitra, the basic nature of a man's self. It's an important aspect of taharah, physical and spiritual purity and cleanliness, which is so strongly emphasized in Islam. When the foreskin is not removed or only partially removed, urine and other secretions can collect under the folded skin. Sometimes it can be the site of painful infections. It is part of the hygiene rules taught by Prophet Muhammad (s) that all Muslims wash with water at the toilet to clean themselves. Muslims can't wash for salah (prayer) unless this prior step is taken to remove filth. Circumcision also reduces the small risk of cancer of the penis.

People have expressed concern about female circumcision. A few Muslim groups in the world have practiced some form of this, as have other groups of people who are not Muslim. It existed in most of those regions before Islam. However, there is no mention in Qur'an of this practice. There is no mention in hadith books that Prophet Muhammad (s) ordered this to be done to any woman or girl. There is no mention of it being done to his daughters, his wives, or his granddaughter, or to any of the women of the companions. There is an overarching legal tradition in Islam that nothing should be done to the body that might harm it.

CONCLUSION

Allah (swt) has sent us guidance in both the Qur'an and the example of Prophet Muhammad (s) to help us follow the best path for raising our children. Allah knew the world of parents in the past and what guidance they needed and He knows the world we live in here and now and what guidance we need. His wisdom is eternal.

With the billions of Muslims who have lived over the centuries, there have been all kinds of successful Muslim parents from all walks of life in countries all over the world, living in tents in a desert, in high rise apartments in large cities, in palaces and on farms in the countryside. Parents have managed through wars, famine, and disease. They have faced every imaginable hardship. With the inspiration from Qur'an and hadith they have persisted.

The great scholar, Imam Bukhari was raised by a single mom. For about four years of his childhood, he was blind from some disease. The story is recounted that his sight was restored because of the prayers of his mother. Other great scholars like Imam Shafi and Imam Ahmed ibn Hanbal were also raised by single mothers and lived through difficult times.

Few parents will see their children become great religious scholars, of course. And if we felt we had to measure our success or failure as a parent based on whether our child became a scholar, we would be in error. The prayers of the prophets for their children were not for their children to become prophets like them. As Prophet Zachariah (s) prayed:

"My Lord, give me a pure and virtuous descendant of my own, for You hear all requests." (Qur'an 3:38).

As with all other things that we do in life, Allah (swt) measures us by our intentions and our efforts. The child He gives us is a gift for which we should rejoice and celebrate. He knows the child He has given us, not the child we imagined perhaps, but the one that He knows is good for us to have. He knows us better than we know ourselves. Children come to us at birth, ready to adapt to us. We will be adapting to them, too. We will

187

share joys and sorrow together as they grow up and we grow in understanding and wisdom.

No book can discuss every issue that will confront the parent. Hopefully the material presented in this book can help to inspire parents to adapt the guiding principles from Qur'an and sunnah to their particular situation.

We can reduce parenting to the simple actions of:

- Modeling the behavior we want our children to learn
- Coaching them to model the behavior until they gradually learn to do it themselves
- Guiding them with simple instruction and rewards
- Managing the environment so that it nurtures their growth and learning

Things don't look too difficult and complicated like this.

Our Prophet (s) encouraged us to value moderation and told us that Allah will answer the prayer of the parent. The Qur'an promises that Allah (swt) will never send us something harder than we can bear. If we try our best and pray to Allah (swt) to cover our faults and errors, Insha Allah, Allah willing, He will accept our efforts and our intentions and reward us for them.

I'll never let the efforts of any of you who made an effort (on behalf of Allah) become lost, be he male or female, for you're equally from each other. (Qur'an 3:195)

BIBLIOGRAPHY

Abd al-Ati, H. *The Family Structure in Islam*, American Trust Publications, Plainfield, IN., 1977.

Aims and Objectives of Islamic Education, chapters 4 and 6. Hodder and Stoughton, U.K., 1980.

Al-Ghazali, Abu Hamid. *Revival of Religious Learning*, Translated by Fazl-ul-Karim, vol. 3 ch. 5. http://www.ghazali.org/ihya/english/

Al-Ghazali, M. *The Muslim's Character*. International Islamic Federation of Student Organizations, Kuwait, 1983.

An-Nawawi's Forty Hadith, translated by Ibrahim, Ezzeddin, Johnson-Davies, Denys, pub by International Islamic Publishing house, Riyad, SA, 1992.

An-Nawawi, Imam Abu Zakariya Yahya bin Sharaf, *Riyadh-us-Saleheen*, translated by S.M. Madni abbasi, International Islamic Publishers LTD. Karachi, Pakistan, 1983.

Arain, Mariam. et. al. Maturation of the adolescent brain, Neuropsychiatr Dis Treat. 2013; 9: 449–461. Published online 2013 Apr 3. doi: 10/2147/NDT.S39776. https://www.ncbi.nlm.nih.gov/pmc/articles/PMC3621648/

Berk, Laura E., *Infants and Children: Prenatal Through Middle Childhood*, Pearson, New York, 1993.

Bransford, J., and Stein, B. *Behavior Therapy*. Harcourt Brace Jovanovich, N. Y., 1987.

Crary, E. *Without Spanking or Spoiling*. Parenting Press, Seattle, Wa. 1979.

Dobson, J. *The Strong Willed Child, Birth Through Adolescence*. Tyndale House Publishers, Wheaton, Ill. 1987.

Elkadi, A., "Muhammad as a Family Man." Al-Ittihad, vol. 19, No.1. The Muslim Students Association. Plainfield. ln., Jan-March 1982. pp. 49-61.

Elzoghbe, Dr. Mohamed, https://www.youtube.com/watch?v=Pgh0xD1OgC8.

Emerick, Yahiya, The Holy Qur'an in Today's English, pub. 2000.

Faber, A., and Mazlish, E., *Siblings Without Rivalry*, W. W. Norton & Co., N. Y., 1987.

Frost, R., and Moore. S. *The Little Boy Book,* pub. Ballantine Books, Clarkson N. Potter, Crown, NY. 1986.

Gibbs, Nancy. "Bringing Up Father," Time Magazine, June 28, 1993, p. 53-61.

Gomaa, Dr. Ali, https://www.youtube.com/watch?v=pY9oLqMkJU4.

Gordon, T. *PET. Parent Effectiveness Training*. New American Library Pub., 1975.

Hadithcollection.com

Hubaiti, A. "The Prophet and Children," Journal of the Muslim World League, Makka, Saudi Arabia, July 1979, pp 25-29.

Ilg, P, and Ames, L. *Child Behavior from Birth to Ten*. Harper & Row, N. Y., 1955.

Joomaye, M. H. "The Muslim Woman: Backbone of the Family." The Muslim World League Journal, Makka, Saudi Arabia, Vol. 13, No. 2, Oct.-Nov. 1985, pp. 38-42.

Leman, K. *Making Children Mind Without Losing Yours*. Power Books, Old Tappan, N.J., 1984.

Lewis, D. *How to Be a Gifted Parent*. Berkley Books, N. Y., N. Y., 1979

McDermott, J. *The Complete Book on Sibling Rivalry*. Putnam Publishing Group, N. Y., 1980.

Malik, *Muwatta' Imam Malik*, translated by Muhammad Rahimuddin, pub by Sh. Muhammad Ashraf, Lahore, Pakistan, 1991.

https://nces.ed.gov/programs/coe/indicator_cgg.asp

The Parents' Manual, prepared by the Women's Committee of the MSA, published by American Trust Publications, 1992.

Qurashi, M. Y. "Tips on Child Socialization for a Minority Family," Al-Ittihad. The Muslim Students Association, Maryland, Oct. - Dec, 1981, pp, 3-13.

Sahih Bukhari

Sahih Muslim

Sunan Abu Dawud

Spock, B. *Raising Children in a Difficult Time*. W. W. Norton and Co., N. Y., 1974.

https://sunnah.com

https://www.wisemuslimwomen.org/wp-content/uploads/2017/10/WISE-UP-Adoption.pdf?fbclid=IwAR1Z7UVvQwApkQkHYVSugueI17gwPrt_yiVXI8_hdi7ZaqSthMiG_nXWDyM

https://yaqeeninstitute.org/omar-suleiman/reviving-a-lost-sunnah-adoption-and-foster-care-in-islam/#.XcA5Q5pKiUk

Zimbardo, Philip G., Johnson, Robert L., Weber, Ann L. *Psychology: Core Concepts*, Pearson, Allyn and Bacon, New York, 2008

INDEX

193